Holiness and Ministry

HOLINESS AND MINISTRY

A Biblical Theology of Ordination

Thomas B. Dozeman

OXFORD

UNIVERSITY PRESS

2008

OXFORD
UNIVERSITY PRESS

Oxford University Press, Inc., publishes works that further
Oxford University's objective of excellence
in research, scholarship, and education.

Oxford   New York
Auckland   Cape Town   Dar es Salaam   Hong Kong   Karachi
Kuala Lumpur   Madrid   Melbourne   Mexico City   Nairobi
New Delhi   Shanghai   Taipei   Toronto

With offices in
Argentina   Austria   Brazil   Chile   Czech Republic   France   Greece
Guatemala   Hungary   Italy   Japan   Poland   Portugal   Singapore
South Korea   Switzerland   Thailand   Turkey   Ukraine   Vietnam

Copyright © 2008 by Oxford University Press, Inc.

Published by Oxford University Press, Inc.
198 Madison Avenue, New York, New York 10016

www.oup.com

Oxford is a registered trademark of Oxford University Press

Library of Congress Cataloging-in-Publication Data
Dozeman, Thomas B.
Holiness and ministry : a biblical theology
of ordination / Thomas B. Dozeman.
p. cm.
Includes bibliographical references.
ISBN 978-0-19-536733-1
1. Ordination.   2. Ordination—Biblical teaching.
3. Pastoral theology.   4. Holiness.   I. Title.
BV683.D69 2008
262'.14—dc22   2007052278

2 4 6 8 9 7 5 3 1

Printed in the United States of America
on acid-free paper

Preface

The subject matter of this book emerged from my teaching at United Theological Seminary in Dayton, Ohio. After teaching for a number of years, I began to hear frequently from graduates that parish ministry lacked vocational focus. My experience was the same as my colleagues', and the topic of the vocation of ordination became an ever-growing concern as we reflected on our mission as a seminary. Our faculty conversations prompted me to explore the biblical literature for guidelines on the vocation of the ordained. The research emerged in the classroom, first tentatively in a course on holiness, and eventually in a more defined course on holiness and ministry, now the title of this volume. The eagerness with which students pursued the topic confirmed the timeliness of the subject matter. This book is the outcome of our research.

The book departs from our coursework in one important way. The classes on holiness and ministry would conclude with each student applying the biblical resources on ordination to his or her specific denominational confessions and standards. With many distinct denominations represented at any one time, this gave rise to a robust ecumenical dialogue. Some traditions emphasize more the priestly function of the ordained, while others embrace the prophetic role of ministry. All students were forced to evaluate the strengths and weaknesses of their denomination's understanding of ordination within the matrix of the biblical tradition. The present volume ends by inviting the reader to undertake this important task. In the end biblical literature can only provide a template for theological reflection on ordination, which must be completed by the study of the theological guidelines within particular Christian traditions.

I would like to thank my colleague Richard L. Eslinger for reading an early draft of this study, and I thank Cynthia Read at Oxford University Press for providing important feedback on the content of the book. Special thanks also to Linda Donnelly, Daniel Gonzalez, and Merryl Sloane for steering the manuscript though the editing process. I warmly dedicate the volume to my students at United Theological Seminary.

Contents

Holiness and Ministry

CHAPTER ONE

Introduction

The Goals

Ordination is an ancient and venerable profession. The records of ordained priests reach back into the earliest periods in the ancient Near East. In Mesopotamian writing, we read of priests serving the sacred by maintaining the temple, performing rituals, and delivering omens in order to care for the gods and to transmit holiness to humans.[1] The same was true in ancient Egypt. The Egyptian priests were essential to the earliest development of Egyptian religion and culture, where they played a crucial role in maintaining cosmic harmony, while also providing contact between the sacred and the profane realms.[2] The focus on the sacred continued in the Canaanite and ancient Israelite religions, where the ordained protected the purity of holiness in the temple, while also mediating its health benefits to profane humans.[3]

The early records of priests indicate the organic relationship between the profession of the ordained and the sacred. Without the realm of the sacred, there would be no profession of ordination. The combining of holiness and ordination is meant to underscore the essential relationship between ordination and the sacred from the earliest records of the profession to the present time. This is the starting point for the following biblical theology of ordination, and we will follow the lead of the ancient priests: Our research must be embedded in broad-based reflection on the nature of holiness in human religious experience.

The dominance of the secular world in the modern era, with its tendency to marginalize the power of the sacred, has presented a significant challenge to the profession of ordination. Larry A. Witham has chronicled well the dilemma of the modern era on the profession of ordained ministry in his book *Who Shall Lead Them? The Future of Ministry in America*. Witham concludes that "at the start of the twenty-first century, both clergy watchers and ministers themselves sense that something is slipping in this great American vocation."[4] Henri J. M. Nouwen sensed the same uneasiness over the vocational identity of the ordained at the close of the twentieth century in the book *In the Name of Jesus: Reflections on Christian Leadership*. He attributed the erosion in ministry to the lack of clear theological reflection on the nature of the vocation. He predicted that "without solid theological reflection, future leaders will be little more than pseudo-psychologists, pseudo-sociologists, [and] pseudo-social workers," who lack vocational identity.[5] The ancient records of the ordained in Mesopotamia, Egypt, Canaan, ancient Israel, and the early Christian church would quickly add that the theological reflection that Nouwen urges is an understanding of the sacred and how it functions in human religious experience. The ancient literature leads directly to the conclusion that there can be no vocational identity of the ordained without knowledge of holiness and the sacred. As a result, my first goal in this study is to construct a biblical theology of ordination that is embedded in broad reflection on the nature of holiness in the biblical literature.

My second goal is to fashion a biblical theology of ordination that is able to serve as a springboard for ecumenical dialogue among different Christian traditions with their divergent views on the nature and function of ordination. The World Council of Churches reinforced the urgent need for a critical, theological, and ecumenical understanding of ordination in *The Faith and Order Paper on Baptism, Eucharist, and Ministry*. The report concluded that ordained ministry is "constitutive for the life and witness of the Church" and that a theological understanding of ordination is crucial for vocational identity and for any progress toward the "mutual recognition of the ordained" in ecumenical dialogue.[6] As a result, the report urged all churches "to examine the forms of ordained ministry and the degree to which [they] are faithful to its original intentions." "Churches," the report concluded, "must be prepared to renew their understanding and their practice of ordained ministry" as they enter into ecumenical dialogue.[7]

Biblical theologians have not responded to the challenge of the World Council of Churches to explore anew the biblical foundations of ordination. There is presently no comprehensive biblical theology of ordination, which could serve as a resource for the formation of clergy in individual traditions of the Christian faith and provide the framework for ecumenical dialogue. Contemporary theologians have responded to the call of the World Council of Churches, but the absence of a comprehensive biblical theology of ordination has forced the authors to place far too much emphasis on the scattered references to the pastoral offices in the New Testament, or to bypass biblical literature altogether by grounding their studies in the theology and ecclesiology of distinct denominations or traditions of the church.

Stephen Sprinkle's *Ordination: Celebrating the Gift of Ministry* provides an example of contemporary theological reflection on ordination.[8] The work is a careful and excellent comparison of the theology, ecclesiology, and rituals of ordination in several denominations. The distinctive views of ordination are related through a series of tensions, including the separation of clergy from laity, the functional as compared to the sacramental view of ministry, ordination as office or as charismatic gift, the role of the ordained as ambassador or servant, and the understanding of ordination as a rite or a process. Although Sprinkle affirms the Bible as "our primary norm for understanding ordination," its role in the study is limited to selected passages from the New Testament, which, in the end, the author rightly concludes provide "no blueprint for ministry."[9]

This book, *Holiness and Ministry: A Biblical Theology of Ordination*, is intended to be an initial response to the call of the World Council of Churches for renewed theological reflection on the biblical roots of ordination. The central teaching on ordination in the Bible is contained in the complex development of the Mosaic office, where the prophetic and priestly dimensions of Moses's call establish the paradigm of ordination to word and sacrament in Christian tradition. The Mosaic office in Torah informs the composition of New Testament literature in dynamic ways, which far exceed the scattered references to pastoral offices, requiring a broad interbiblical approach to the study of ordination.

The Methodology

In this book I will relate three methodologies: (1) the history of religions and the study of holiness; (2) the history of the composition of the Pentateuch and the interpretation of the Mosaic office in Torah; and (3) canonical criticism and the interbiblical interpretation of the Mosaic office. The interweaving of the three methodologies will illustrate the dynamic way in which the Mosaic office in Torah provides the biblical foundation for the ordination to word and sacrament in Christian tradition.

Holiness and the History of Religions

God and holiness form an intricate web in the Bible, signifying the separateness of the deity from profane human experience. Ordination in the Bible derives from the holiness of God, since the ordained assist in bridging the separation between a holy God and profane humans. For this reason, a biblical theology of ordination requires a thorough understanding of the holiness of God and its influence on human life and worship practice. Mircea Eliade's broad research on holiness in the history of religions will provide the background for interpreting two distinct theories of holiness in biblical literature: as a dynamic force and as a ritual resource.[10] Rudolf Otto's classic *The Idea of the Holy* will illustrate the quality of holiness as the numinous, which is conceived as a dynamic force that directly invades humans.[11] Jacob Milgrom's anthropological research on holiness in his Leviticus commentary will illustrate the ritual character of holiness as a sacramental resource.[12] The goal of this aspect of the study will be to demonstrate that the two theories of holiness, as dynamic force and as ritual resource, establish the paradigm of ordination to word and sacrament in Christian tradition.

The Mosaic Office and the History of the Composition of Torah

The research in the modern era on the composition of the Torah has demonstrated that the priestly literature and the Book of Deuteronomy represent competing groups in the late monarchical and the second temple periods of Judaism, with distinctive views of the sacred, cultic practice, and ordination.[13] We will not review the rich history of interpretation that has led to the identification of the distinct religious movements in ancient Israel and their divergent bodies of literature. Our study will follow a broad consensus in which the description of the Tabernacle in Exodus 25–31 and 35–40; the cultic ritual in the book of Leviticus; and the campsite in Numbers 1–10 are assigned to priestly tradition and contrasted to the Book of Deuteronomy. Our focus will be on the contrasting views of holiness and ordination in these distinct bodies of literature.

This study will clarify that the contrasting traditions of holiness in the priestly literature and in the book of Deuteronomy give rise to conflicting portraits of Moses in the Torah as a prophet and as a priest. The book of Deuteronomy advances a theology of holiness as a dynamic force, which is represented as a voice that invades Moses at Mount Horeb, resulting in his idealization as an inspired teacher of the divine word. The priestly literature advances a theology of holiness as a ritual resource, which is made available to Moses and to Israel through the fiery glory of Yahweh, which eventually descends into the altar of the Tabernacle. The transfer of holiness in the priestly literature requires that Moses function as a priest, who performs ritual mediation through sacrifices. Our focus of interpretation will be less on the character of Moses than on the authoritative offices of leadership which he represents.[14] We will see that the competing portraits of Moses as prophetic teacher and as priestly mediator combine to form the Mosaic office in Torah.

There are three goals in the study of the history of the composition of the Mosaic office in Torah. The first is to distinguish the divergent views of holiness and the competing portraits of Moses's leadership in the priestly literature and in the book of Deuteronomy, which combine to form the Mosaic office in the composition of the Torah. Chapter 4 will describe the presentation of Moses as an interpreter of the divine word in Deuteronomy, while chapter 5 will explore the portrayal of Moses as a priest and ritual specialist in the priestly literature. The second goal is to relate the distinctive offices of Moses with the two theories of holiness that emerge from the study of the history of religions. The third goal is to demonstrate that the distinctive traditions of ordination in the Mosaic office cannot be harmonized with each other. The result is that the Mosaic office in Torah holds in tension two theories of holiness and two views of ordination, which lays the foundation for the interpretation of ordination to word and sacrament in Christian tradition.

Canonical Criticism and the Interbiblical Interpretation of the Mosaic Office

Canonical criticism will provide the lens to explore the ongoing influence of the Mosaic office in Christian tradition. The methodology will clarify the way in which the twofold character of the Mosaic office influences the formation of the New Testament literature and lays the foundation for the interpretation of ordination to word and sacrament in Christian tradition. The portrayal of Moses as prophet and priest in the Torah does not exhaust the imagery of ordination in the New Testament nor in Christian tradition, where the metaphors of the king in the Psalms, the suffering servant in Isaiah, or the sage in the Wisdom literature also influence the emerging understanding of the ordained in the early church.[15] Yet, the idealization of Moses as a prophetic teacher of the divine word and as the priestly mediator of sacramental rituals plays a prominent role in the understanding of the office of ordination in Christian tradition. A brief description of canonical criticism as it has been developed by Brevard S. Childs and James A. Sanders will clarify the hermeneutical perspective, which will inform the interbiblical interpretation of the Mosaic office.[16]

   Canonical criticism is a historical-critical methodology focused on the late formation of biblical texts by religious communities, which attributed divine authority to the literature. Canonical criticism is concerned with the dynamic relationships among a religiously authoritative text, the faith community that preserved it, and the influence of the text on the religious life of future communities of faith. The methodology investigates the unique literary features and the social function of the genre of canon, paying particular attention to the way in which once historically conditioned literature is given a new authoritative function as the comprehensive word of God to later communities of faith. Two central presuppositions guide canonical criticism, which will also influence our interpretation of the Mosaic office. First, the religious perspective of those who shaped the literature becomes an important feature in interpretation. Thus, faith and the realm of the sacred become crucial hermeneutical components in the critical interpretation of canonical literature.[17] Second, canonical literature is intended for the religious use of faith communities through time.[18] The aim of canonical literature, therefore, is not simply to preserve the past, but to speak directly to future readers about the ongoing power of the sacred in human religious experience.

   The Mosaic office provides an illustration of the methodology of canonical criticism. The conflicting idealizations of Moses in the priestly literature and in the book of Deuteronomy certainly provide glimpses into the social history of ancient Israel in the late monarchical and second temple periods, when prophetic and priestly groups competed for authority by embedding their models of leadership in the characterization of Moses. The methodologies of historical criticism and the history of the composition of the Pentateuch seek to clarify the social history of this period. But the canonical critic would add that the religious authority of the Torah does not arise from its historical reliability concerning the central character, Moses, nor from the recovery of the social world of the authors. When the Mosaic office is read from the perspective of canonical criticism, it would be a mistake to interpret the Torah as though it were shaped simply to preserve the social world of ancient Israel.

The methodology of canonical criticism emphasizes that the Torah is constructed to speak directly to future readers about the ongoing power of holiness in the Mosaic office. The community that shaped the story of Torah was certainly interested in the social forces which influenced the portrayal of Moses, but the active role of faith in the composition of canonical literature necessarily loosened the Torah from the past so that it could function as divine, authoritative literature for future readers. The result is that the meaning of the Torah was not confined to the past, but extended into the ongoing religious life of the Jewish community in the second temple period. And, as an emerging form of Judaism, the early church adopted the same perspective, also attributing divine authority to the Torah, with the result that the Mosaic office influenced the composition of the New Testament and the understanding of ordination to word and sacrament in early Christian tradition. Thus, a canonical interpretation of the Mosaic office must be aware of the adaptable character of canonical literature by ongoing communities of faith. For this reason, I will refer at times to the ordination stories of Moses in the priestly literature and in the book of Deuteronomy with the Christian terms of word and sacrament, even though these designations are clearly anachronistic for Jewish literature in the second temple period.[19]

Canonical criticism also allows for an ecumenical interpretation of ordination, which we will explore in the final chapter of the study. The distinct theories of holiness and the two interpretations of the Mosaic office accentuate the pluralism of the biblical teaching on ordination within historically dissimilar traditions. The canonical interpretation of ordination will build on the pluralism of historical criticism, while changing the focus from the distinct traditions of the Mosaic office to their multiple literary relationships in the formation of the canon. Thus, canonical criticism raises the question of how distinct religious groups, which adhere to canon, are able to hear the voice of the same God through historically dissimilar traditions.[20]

Two features of canonical criticism will provide a broad ecumenical resource for the contemporary study of ordination. First, the interpretation will illustrate a range of possible literary relationships between word and sacrament, illustrating the insight of Brevard S. Childs that the role of canon is to provide the boundaries of possible interpretations of ordination, rather than to harmonize the distinct forms of the Mosaic office into a unified reading.[21] Second, canonical criticism also accentuates the dynamic relationship between a fixed canon and the faith communities that preserve and use it, which is characterized by James A. Sanders as the adaptability of canon.[22] The adaptability of canon underscores the inevitability of diverse interpretations of ordination to word and sacrament in distinct Christian communities, which cannot help but relate the prophetic and priestly aspects of the Mosaic office differently in light of their unique religious experience. The controlled pluralism of canonical criticism will provide a response to the World Council of Church's call to explore anew the biblical foundations of ordination. The goal of this aspect of the study is to fashion a biblical theology of ordination for distinct communities of faith, which can also function as a broad foundation for the mutual understanding of ordination in ecumenical dialogue.

The Overview

Chapters 2 and 3 will establish the foundation for our study of ordination. Chapter 2 will explore the organic relationship between holiness and ordination, while chapter 3 will describe the ways in which biblical authors used the story of Moses to fashion a theology of ordination. In chapter 2, we will describe how holiness is an essential life-giving characteristic of God, which exists in a separate realm from humans. We will explore how the separation gives rise to the distinction between the sacred and the profane in human religious experience. We will see that the need to bridge the gap between the sacred and the profane gives rise to the profession of ordination. Our study will clarify that the distribution of holiness takes place for the most part in the sanctuary and that its transfer can occur through persuasive speech or rituals. The two means by which holiness is transferred to humans define the parameters of the profession of ordination to word and sacrament. Chapter 3 will illustrate how the biblical authors used the story of Moses to model ordination, which we have characterized as the Mosaic office. The dynamic relationship between holiness and the Mosaic office provides the central teaching on ordination in biblical literature.

Chapters 4 and 5 explore the structure of the Mosaic office in Torah as the model for the ordination to word and sacrament in Christian tradition. Chapters 2 and 3 underscore that ordination to the Mosaic office emerges from broad theories of holiness, which include comprehensive world views about the separation of the sacred and the profane, the danger of the sacred to the profane world, and how these distinct realms may be safely bridged by the selection of ordained leaders. Chapter 4 will investigate the theology of holiness in the book of Deuteronomy in order to interpret the ordination to the divine word, which Moses models in his role as the prophetic teacher. We will trace the same theology of holiness in selected New Testament literature. Chapter 5 will explore the role of Moses as a mediator of holiness through rituals in the priestly literature and its influence in the formation of selected New Testament texts. We will see that the theologies of ordination in the book of Deuteronomy and in the priestly literature arise from the twofold character of holiness as a dynamic force and as a ritual resource.

Chapters 6 and 7 will explore the role of the Mosaic office in fashioning a biblical theology of ordination to word and sacrament in Christian tradition. Chapter 6 will focus exclusively on the offices of the ordained in the New Testament literature. We will see that the New Testament authors did not provide a fully developed theology of ordination for the emerging church and that the references to the ordained presuppose the more extensive theological reflection on holiness and ordination within the Mosaic office. Our study of the office of ordination in the New Testament will reinforce the need for a broad view of biblical authority, in which the primary teaching on ordination remains in the Hebrew scripture, rather than in the New Testament. Chapter 7 will turn to the contemporary challenges facing the ordained. We will examine how the Mosaic office provides guidelines for candidates of ordination to discern their call experience and to establish professional identity. We will conclude our study by examining how the Mosaic office provides both a resource for the formation of clergy within individual traditions of Christianity and the basis for a broad ecumenical biblical theology of ordination.

CHAPTER TWO

Holiness and Ordination

Ordination for ministry derives from the holiness of God. If God were not holy, there would be no such thing as religion in human experience, nor would there be any need for a select group of ordained persons to work in the service of the sacred. For this reason, a theology of ordination requires a thorough understanding of the holiness of God and its influence on human life. In this chapter, we will interpret the nature of holiness from three different perspectives. First, we will describe how holiness is an essential characteristic of God, whose root meaning, separation, gives rise to the distinction between the sacred and the profane in human religious experience. Second, we will explore the important role of sanctuaries for relating the sacred and the profane in religious experience, and the need for the ordained to undergo a rite of passage to work within the realm of the sacred. Third, we will investigate two theories of holiness, as a dynamic power and as a ritual resource, which inform all biblical theologies of ordination.

Holiness as Separation

God and holiness form an intricate web in the Bible. God is the source of all holiness. Yahweh is "the Holy One of Israel," proclaims the prophet Isaiah (Is 1:4). The Song of the Sea echoes the words of the prophet, celebrating Yahweh as "majestic in holiness" (Ex 15:11). The cherubim chant in the Jerusalem temple: "Holy, holy, holy is Yahweh of hosts" (Is 6:3). God is described as the "Holy Father" in the Gospel of John (17:11).

The biblical texts make it abundantly clear that holiness is a quality that emanates directly from the character or essence of God. Jacob Milgrom writes: "Holiness is his [God's] quintessential nature, distinguishing him from all beings."[1] But holiness cannot be equated with God. Rather, holiness acts as an agency of the divine will. The divine command "You shall be holy, for I am holy" (Lv 11:45) illustrates the distinction between God and holiness. The command is directed to the Israelites in Leviticus 11:45 and to Christians in 1 Peter 1:15–16. The command is not for the Israelites or the Christians to become God, but to be holy. Holiness and God are inseparable in the Bible, but they are not the same. The subtle relationship between God and holiness is crucial for understanding biblical religion and ordination.

The root meaning of "holiness" (*qodesh*), according to David Wright, is "to be separate."[2] The verbal form of the word, "to be holy" (*qadash*), illustrates the root meaning. The verb first appears at the close of the creation story in Genesis 1 in the establishment of a sabbath as a distinct day from the previous six days. Genesis 2:3 states: "God blessed the seventh day and *hallowed it*" (*qadash*). Although the verb is correctly translated "to consecrate" or "to make hallow," the root meaning is that God "separated" the sabbath from the other six days, thus creating a permanent distinction between them. The first six days of creation focus on the human world in all of its complexity. But on the seventh day, no act of creation takes place and no object within creation demands the reader's attention. The focus is instead on God, who is described as resting in the divine realm, prompting worship (= sacred activity) in the human world. The holiness of the seventh day introduces a different quality of experience, which indicates a separation between God and the entire creation, including human existence. The separation of holiness gives rise to the confession that God is transcendent, "the other," meaning separate from us and from our created world. The prophet Hosea gives voice to the separate quality of holiness with the divine proclamation: "I am God and not human" (Hos 11:9).

The Sacred and the Profane

The divine quality of holiness introduces two types of separation between God and humans.[3] The first is the separation between the sacred and the profane. We might call this an ontological distinction. The sacred is the immortal world of God, and holiness is intrinsic to God. Hannah gives expression to the intrinsic quality of holiness in God and to the separation of the sacred and the profane in 1 Samuel 2:2 when she prays: "There is no Holy One except Yahweh, no one besides you" (see also Is 5:24; Ps 89:18). The writer of 1 Peter echoes the thoughts of Hannah: "He [God] who called you is holy" (1 Pt 1:15). Holiness can also be a characteristic of the region of heaven, when biblical writers declare it to be the dwelling place of God. The psalmist confesses: "Now I know that Yahweh will help his anointed; he will answer him from his holy heaven" (Ps 20:6). The throne vision in Revelation 4 also weaves together images of the holy God enthroned in heaven.

The profane is the mortal world of humans. Holiness is absent in this world. The creation story in Genesis 1 illustrates the separation of the sacred and the profane. Humans are good, blessed, and even image-bearers of God in the utopian world of Genesis 1, but they are not holy (Gn 1:26–30). The same is true for all other aspects of creation in Genesis 1. The created world is good, but not holy (Gn 1:31). God is qualitatively distinct from humans and the created world in Genesis 1. And, as we have already seen, holiness is only introduced on the seventh day, as a moment in time, not as an object within creation. The message of Genesis 1 is clear. The sacred and the profane are inherently different from each other. They are not to be mixed, not even in the utopian world of Genesis 1. The prophet Isaiah agrees, when he speaks for Yahweh, the Holy One: "My thoughts are not your thoughts, neither are your ways my ways" (Is 55:8).

Mircea Eliade characterizes the separation between the sacred and the profane as "two modes of being in the world," which give rise to two different qualities of experience.[4] The first six days of creation represent the diversity of our world, with each of the first six days describing different aspects of creation, including light (day one), air (day two), water (day three), the heavenly bodies (day four), plants (day five), and animals (day six). But Eliade would argue that the diversity of the created world is of the same quality of experience, since all aspects of the profane world are commonly shared features of human life. Eliade employs the metaphor of geometry to describe the similarity of experience in the profane world, since geometrical space can be cut and delimited in any direction without qualitative differentiation. Profane experience, like geometry, is "homogeneous space."

Eliade's notion of homogeneous space requires further description. Homogeneous space does not mean that all human experience is the

same, nor that it can be reduced to a limited number of shared characteristics. Rather, there is a vast diversity of human experience in homogeneous space, depending on our ethnicity, gender, and cultural
context, among other factors. What homogeneous space does mean is
that, as humans, we are able to share to some degree in each other's
experience and world view. It is possible for men and women or different
races to communicate and to influence each other. The resources for this
communication reside in the profane world of humans; they do not
require a divine revelation. The experience of traveling provides an
illustration. Any person who travels to another country is overwhelmed
by the new experience. The food is different. The language is incom-
prehensible. The climate is on an unfamiliar cycle. And the daily habits
and customs of the people are strange. Yet, over time, we can learn a new
language, change our eating habits, and adjust to a new pattern of life.
The bridging of human cultures is possible, according to Eliade, because
there is a shared quality to human experience in the profane world. Thus,
homogeneous space is in many respects relative, which means that it lacks
a point of orientation within the profane world. The result of the rela-
tivity of homogeneous space is that there is no central experience or
location by which to evaluate or to arrange the rich diversity within the
created world.

Eliade argues that the qualitative contrast to the rich diversity of
profane experience is the sacred. The sacred is a different mode of experience altogether from the homogeneous space of the profane world.
As such, the invasion of the sacred is able to provide orientation in the
diversity of the profane world. The seventh day provides an example of
the qualitatively distinct experience of the sacred from the profane world
of the first six days. In Genesis 1, the different quality of experience is
characterized as human rest, which mimics the activity of God. Eliade
would characterize the sabbath rest as an irruption of the sacred into the
more homogeneous experience of the profane world, which is represented by the first six days of creation. The result is that the sabbath
becomes the point of orientation in Genesis 1 for evaluating the other six
days of creation. The invasion of the kingdom of God in the New
Testament serves the same purpose as the sabbath. Its hidden and mys-
terious quality separates the kingdom of God from the profane world,
while also providing a new orientation to those who enter it (Mk 4).

The necessary separation of the sacred and the profane is stressed in
Luke 11:14–23, when the kingdom of God is contrasted to the kingdom

of Satan. The separation is illustrated even better at the outset of the flood story (Gn 6–9). The merging of the two realms through sexual inter-course between gods and humans, which gives birth to the Nephilim ("the fallen ones"), is stated as one of the reasons that God destroys the world (Gn 6:1–4). The flood graphically portrays the consequences of trespass between the sacred and the profane. All orientation is lost when the sacred and the profane merge in the birth of the Nephilim, and, as a consequence, the world returns to water.

The Pure and the Impure

The second level of separation arising from holiness is more environ-mental, biological, and social than ontological. This separation is the result of violence entering the human world. Humans are not only separated from God because of their profane and mortal nature, they are also separated through contamination or pollution, represented most clearly by the shedding of blood in the story of Cain and Abel (Gn 4). The shedding of blood in this story is a virus, which originates from the human ego. The incubation period begins when Cain experiences anger over the divine acceptance of Abel's sacrifice, rather than his own. The deity warns Cain to control his ego and his anger, stating: "If you do well, will you not be accepted? And if you do not do well, sin is lurking at the door; its desire is for you, but you must master it" (Gn 4:7).

Violence is rooted in the human will in the story of Cain. God encourages Cain not to limit his view of the "other" simply through the lens of his own ego. Cain fails the test and kills his brother, which transforms violence from a test of the human ego into a virus within creation. The virus of violence enters the created world when the blood of Abel leaves his body and is absorbed into the ground as a result of Cain's act of murder. Once the blood of Abel penetrates the ground, it becomes a pollutant in creation, rather than a life force in his body. Blood out of context—that is to say, blood outside of the human body—is the starting point for all violence in the world. The biblical writer under-scores the changed situation by noting that the blood screams out to God upon its contact with the ground (Gn 4:10). Even though Cain alone commits the act of murder, the result is the permanent pollution of creation. Blood in the ground is like radiation poisoning. Once it is in the soil, it permanently contaminates the environment, including all social dimensions of human life. Radiation poisoning will inevitably enter the body of anyone born within the scope of its contamination. The inevitable result is social violence, which, according to the author of Genesis 4:17–26, is at the root of all human civilization. By attributing music, industry, and all forms of manufacturing to the genealogy of Cain, the biblical writer is stating that even the most beautiful creations of human society are built on a foundation of blood. They must not be mistaken for the utopian world of Genesis 1.

The violent shedding of Abel's blood creates a further separation between God and humans. The biblical writers use a range of terms to characterize this further state of alienation. Now, humans are not only mortal (profane), they are also diseased, which is expressed through the biblical language of impurity, or violence. The result of the diseased or violent state of humans is the further separation from the deity, beyond the sacred and the profane.[5] The biological distinction attributes purity, life, health, wholeness, order, and peace to divine holiness as compared to the impure and violent world of death, disease, decay, and social disorder that has now infected creation and all humans. The result is that humans are removed from holiness in two ways: through the contrast between the sacred and the profane and through the additional separation between the pure and the impure. Jacob Milgrom illustrates the two-part separation with the diagram in figure 2.1.[6]

The categories of the sacred and the profane in the top level of the diagram represent the ontological separation between God and creation. The categories of the pure and the impure in the lower level of the diagram designate the environmental contrast between holiness as health and the contamination of our world from the violence of the human ego. When the four categories—sacred, profane, pure, impure—are brought together as in the diagram, a new contrast emerges. The sacred in the top level and the impure in the lower level cross over to create a volatile contrast. The reason is that impurity is a dynamic force that is able to act against the power of the sacred. The two active forces, the sacred and the impure, create an explosive mixture because they cannot occupy the same space—one must drive the other away.

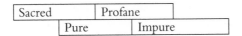

FIGURE 2.1

The introduction of impurity in the form of human violence widens the distance between God and humans. Humans are described as contagious or as an abomination to God, prompting divine anger. Some biblical authors describe the divine anger with analogies to human emotions. Thus, Moses warns the Israelites of Yahweh's anger in Deuteronomy 4:2: "For Yahweh your God is a devouring fire, a jealous God." Other biblical writers characterize the anger of God with the medical imagery of a plague, whose antidote is the proper priestly ritual. Numbers 16:46 states: "Moses said to Aaron, 'Take your censer, put fire on it from the altar and lay incense on it, and carry it quickly to the congregation and make atonement for them. For the wrath has gone out from Yahweh; the plague has begun.'" Statements such as that of the apostle Paul in Romans 1:18 could be interpreted in either direction: "For the wrath of God is revealed from heaven against all ungodliness and wickedness of those who by their wickedness suppress the truth."

The two-part separation between God and humans makes any contact between them volatile and dangerous. Unregulated contact with holiness results in death to humans, regardless of motive. God kills Uzzah when he steadies the ark (a holy object), in spite of his good intention (2 Sm 6:6–11). We might compare the action against Uzzah with electricity in the modern world. Electricity is a power that is able to provide light for entire cities. But it will kill any human who touches it unprotected. Obviously, the ancients did not yet have the experience of electricity. But they did know fire. And in the ancient world, fire often represents the danger of holiness. Fire accompanies gods in the ancient Near East in the form of the *melammu*, a radiant halo surrounding the head of a god, carried over into Christian art in the portrayal of Jesus.[7] Fire can represent divine judgment, as in the plague cycle, when Yahweh, in the form of the storm God, rained down hail and lightning on the Egyptians (Ex 9:13–35). The same fire can purify a human, as in the case of the prophet Isaiah, who declares himself unclean and in danger of death in the presence of God, but is then purged by the holy fire from the altar (Is 6:1–5). The imagery of the prophet Isaiah is carried over in the New Testament story of Pentecost, where fire also invades the apostles (Acts 2:1–4).

The two-part separation between God and humans results in a paradoxical situation. Humans need holiness for life and health. This is illustrated in the stories of the prophet Isaiah and the apostles in the book of Acts. But the gift is a two-edged sword. It can kill or heal.[8] Thus, humans do well to proceed with great caution, as in the case of the prophet Isaiah, who proclaims when confronted by holiness: "Woe is me! I am lost, for I am a man of unclean lips, and I live among a people of unclean lips; yet my eyes have seen the king, Yahweh of hosts!" (Is 6:5). The most appropriate human response to holiness is fear or awe, as modeled by Moses before the burning bush in Exodus 3:6: "Moses hid his face, for he was afraid to look at God."[9] The same fear overwhelms Zechariah, when he is confronted by the angel Gabriel in Luke 1:12: "When Zechariah saw [the angel of Yahweh], he was terrified; and fear overwhelmed him."

The volatile nature of holiness in human experience underscores that biblical confessions, such as "Immanuel" ("God with Us") or "Yahweh, the Holy One in our midst," are filled with unresolved tension, giving rise to a central theme in biblical literature: How is God able to overcome the separation inherent in holiness, take up residency on earth, and renew the world without destroying humans? The goal of biblical religion is to overcome the separation between God and humans, the sacred and the profane, and ultimately to overcome the violence that originates from the human ego, which pollutes the earth and alienates humans from God.

Holiness, Sanctuaries, and Ordination as a Rite of Passage

The problem of bridging the gap between the sacred and the profane is both spatial (heaven and earth) and qualitative (divine and human). Our aim in this book is to explore the second problem, the qualitative difference between a holy God and a profane and violent people, since it clarifies the need for ordained persons to mediate holiness between God and humans. But before turning to an examination of ordination, we would do well to explore in more detail the spatial problem of holiness, represented by the separation between heaven and earth, since it highlights the important role of the sanctuary as the place of holiness on earth and as the work setting of the ordained.

The emphasis on the sanctuary, as the location of the sacred on earth, is crucial for any person who is reflecting on a career in ordained ministry. It indicates that the workplace for the ordained is the sanctuary and not the world at large. To be sure, the ordained cannot be restricted to the sanctuary and must become ethical agents of holiness throughout the

profane world. Yet the sanctuary remains the home office for the ordained. Just as in other professions, employees cannot confine their jobs
to the office, but must interact with other persons and firms around the
world, so must the clergy represent the sacred in all areas of the profane
world. But the home office for the world mission of ethics and justice is
the sanctuary.

The interpretation of sanctuaries as sacred places on earth is developed through the imagery of the cosmic mountain throughout biblical
literature. In the Bible, the gulf between heaven and earth is bridged by
the descent of God to the summit of a mountain. Exodus 19:16–19
provides an example. The entrance of Yahweh into the created world to
meet with the Israelite people in the wilderness is described as a descent to
the summit of Mount Sinai. The same imagery repeats in the transfiguration story of Jesus, which takes place on a high mountain (Mk 9:2–13).
The episodes illustrate that mountains often symbolize the meeting of
heaven and earth. R. E. Clements concluded that, when mountains take
on the symbolic role of representing the descent and presence of a holy
God on earth, they become "cosmic mountains," because their summit
symbolizes the touching of heaven and earth.[10] The descent of God to
the summit of a cosmic mountain is often accompanied by a *theophany*
("appearance of God"), which includes fire, lightning, thunder, and
earthquakes. Exodus 19:16–19 once again provides an illustration: There
is thunder and lightning, while the mountain is "wrapped in smoke,
because Yahweh had descended upon it in fire; the smoke went up like
the smoke of a kiln, while the whole mountain shook violently." Mount
Sinai is a cosmic mountain, because it becomes the holy mountain of
residency for Yahweh and must, therefore, be safeguarded from the
profane world of the Israelites. Yahweh states to Moses: "Set limits
around the mountain and keep it holy [i.e., separate]" (Ex 19:23).

Mount Sinai is not the only mountain home of Yahweh. Deuteronomy 5:2 locates the same event on Mount Horeb, when Moses states:
"Yahweh our God made a covenant with us at Horeb." Psalm 48 cele-
brates the residency of Yahweh on Mount Zion in Jerusalem: "Great is
Yahweh and greatly to be praised in the city of our God. His holy
mountain, beautiful in elevation, is the joy of all the earth, Mount Zion,
in the far north, the city of the great king." Psalm 99:9 echoes Psalm 48:
"Extol Yahweh our God, and worship at his holy mountain; for Yahweh
our God is holy." The setting of the mountain as a channel for the sacred

invasion into the profane world continues into the New Testament, with the Sermon on the Mount in the Gospel of Matthew (Mt 5).

The mountains of revelation throughout the Bible are associated with specific temples or distinctive forms of worship. Mount Zion is the location for the Jerusalem temple, where the enthronement of God is closely tied to the sacramental rituals that celebrate the power of the king. Mount Sinai is the setting for the priestly Tabernacle in Exodus 25–31, where Yahweh mediates holiness by means of priests who perform sacramental rituals. Mount Horeb is associated with the tent of meeting in the book of Deuteronomy, where Yahweh transmits holiness through teachers of scripture. Each of these sanctuaries represents the presence of Yahweh on earth, although they advocate different forms of worship. The correlation between sanctuaries and the imagery of the cosmic mountain, reaching to heaven, continues in the New Testament. Peter's first response to the transfiguration of Jesus, for example, is to build sanctuaries on the mountain. We continue to see the influence of this tradition in church architecture through the prominent role of steeples, which also indicate that the building touches heaven and is, therefore, able to transmit holiness into its space.

The association of sanctuaries and cosmic mountains is important for our study of ordination. Sanctuaries overcome the spatial separation between heaven and earth. And in achieving this goal, sanctuaries are transformed into holy places (cosmic mountains). As a location of holiness in the profane world, the sanctuary provides the setting for preaching and for sacramental resources that achieve human health and wholeness. Thus, the sanctuary is the home office for the ordained. As a sacred place, the sanctuary is the resource for all power in ministry, both for worship in its space and for ethics in the profane world. Psalm 46:4 proclaims the good news that living water flows from the throne of God in the Jerusalem temple on Mount Zion. Exodus 29:43 states the divine promise that the glory of Yahweh will reside in the Tabernacle and sanctify the sanctuary so that the Israelites may come to the knowledge of Yahweh. Deuteronomy 4:10–14 declares that Yahweh spoke to the Israelite people at Mount Horeb and wrote the Decalogue, which instills proper fear in the people. The presence of God is described differently in each case. Yet all of the texts emphasize the setting of the mountain, suggesting the close relationship between holiness and the sanctuary.[11] My colleague Richard L. Eslinger describes the locations of cultic spirituality as "thin places," since they are characterized by a porous membrane between the sacred and the profane.

The accounts of revelation agree that the distribution of holiness in a safe manner will require a select group to give up the freedom of the profane world through the process of ordination in order to work in the service of holiness within the setting of the sanctuary. Thus, sanctuaries emerge as a primary work setting for the ordained. The meaning of the Latin *ordinare* is "to put in order, arrange, prepare." The ordained are those who prepare and arrange the sacred world of the sanctuary in order to mediate holiness to other humans. This work may be through the serving of the sacraments or in the interpretation of the divine word. In so doing, the ordained assist in bridging the qualitative gap between a holy God and profane humans.

The role of the ordained to serve in the sanctuary indicates that the process of ordination requires a rite of passage, in which candidates undergo transition from the profane world to the sacred. A. van Gennep defined a *rite of passage* as a ritual means of transition by which a person is carried from one phase of human experience to another.[12] The transfer of a human during the ritual process of ordination from the profane world to the sacred realm of the sanctuary certainly fulfills the description of a rite of passage.

Van Gennep described the structure of a rite of passage as consisting of three phases.[13] The first phase is the act of separation from a social structure or cultural condition. In the process of ordination, the act of separation is often initiated by a call experience, which candidates for ministry often describe as a life-changing disruption of a previously established way of life. The second phase of a rite of passage is the transitional stage, when a person is outside of recognized social structures. The transitional phase is also described as the marginal or liminal state in a rite of passage. The latter word derives from the Latin *limen*, meaning "threshold." Victor Turner characterizes liminality as a time of ambiguity, when participants in a rite of passage are betwixt and between recognized social structures, and thus momentarily free of past constraints. The liminal phase in a rite of passage is a time of training and testing, where participants enter as a tabula rasa in order to undergo initiation, experience role reversals, and create community.[14] The liminal phase in the rite of passage for candidates seeking ordination is a time of education, discernment, and oversight by judicatories. Once the transitional period is complete, the third phase of a rite of passage is the reincorporation of the participant into the new world. The reincorporation, according to Victor and Edith Turner, "installs the person, inwardly transformed and outwardly changed, in a new place in society."[15] For candidates of ordination, the third phase of the rite of passage is the ordination ceremony, which allows the person to undertake service in the sacred space of the sanctuary. But, as also noted by the Turners, traces of the transitional quality of liminality remain in professional religious orders, since the ordained bridge the gap between a sacred God and profane humans. Thus, transitioning between the sacred and the profane becomes a permanent condition for those who undergo ordination.

Two Theories of Holiness and the Ordination to the Divine Word and to Sacramental Rituals

Most Christian traditions ordain clergy into two roles or offices. The two offices are indicated by the phrase "ordination to word and sacrament." The meaning of the phrase varies widely in distinct denominations, yet the two-part character of ordination tends to be a constant feature in most discussions of ordination. The designation of ordination as "word" and "sacrament" arises from the dual character of holiness as a dynamic force and as a ritual resource. The dynamic character of holiness is conceived as a power that directly invades humans. It provides the background for interpreting the ordination to the divine word in Christian tradition, which is often associated loosely with a prophetic office. The ritual character of holiness is the basis for the Christian ordination to sacramental rituals, associated more closely with the priesthood. The two characteristics of holiness are in such profound tension with each other that they cannot be harmonized. Yet, any person pursuing a professional career in ministry must become thoroughly familiar with the dual character of holiness and its implications for the ordination to divine word and sacramental rituals, since ordained persons are required, in most cases, to channel holiness to humans charismatically through the spoken word and ritually through sacramental liturgies.

An understanding of the way in which the dual character of holiness shapes ordination will require careful interpretation of the ordination documents within a specific denomination, which is outside the scope of this study. The goal of this section is more general. It is to clarify the dual character of holiness as a dynamic force and as a ritual resource by examining two contrasting contemporary studies of holiness. The two guides will be Rudolf Otto and Jacob Milgrom. Rudolf Otto wrote *The Idea of the Holy* in the early part of the twentieth century (1917). Otto explored the dynamic power of holiness to counter what he saw as the humanizing of God and religious experience, which had come to dominate the church of his time. The reason, according to Otto, was an overemphasis on the rational nature of religion as a system of moral behavior. For Otto, morality could not be equated with holiness, since holiness was a power in its own right. Jacob Milgrom wrote *Leviticus: A New Translation with Introduction and Commentary* at the close of the twentieth century (1991, 2000, 2001). The negative judgment of ritualized religious practice prompted Milgrom to explore the active power of holiness, which is mediated through sacramental ritual. For Milgrom, rituals, which are empowered by holiness, are anything but merely mechanical rites.

A brief review of Otto's *The Idea of the Holy* will clarify the meaning of holiness as a dynamic power. A summary of Milgrom's *The Leviticus Commentary* will aid in understanding the character of holiness as a ritual resource. Both studies will be summarized in three parts: (1) the separate quality of holiness; (2) the sacred and the profane; and (3) the sacred and ordination. The two contemporary studies will provide the background for interpreting the dual character of holiness in the ordination to word and sacrament within biblical literature.

Rudolf Otto and the Charismatic Power of Holiness

THE SEPARATE QUALITY OF HOLINESS. The primary meaning of holiness for Otto is "to be separate." He described holiness frequently as the "wholly other." But Otto stressed that the separate quality of holiness should not be conceived as a transcendent description of God, who dwells in the sacred realm of heaven far removed from the profane world of humans. Such a view of holiness is too impersonal, according to Otto. When holiness is viewed so impersonally, it provides the background for the theological understanding of holiness as "moral goodness," which humans could observe on earth in order to transfer its sacred quality into the profane world. Otto was convinced that moral systems could not be equated with holiness, because holiness as moral goodness lacks personal power. When holiness is reduced to moral goodness, humans become the dynamic power in its realization within the profane world by adhering to moral codes. The result is the reduction of religion to the social and political organization of the profane world, which too often merges the church and the state into a national or civil religion based on a shared moral code, which is mistakenly given divine authority. For Otto, holiness is first and foremost a dynamic power in its own right, which cannot be reduced simply to a moral system of goodness or justice.[16]

Otto highlighted the dynamic power of holiness by naming it "the numinous." The name derives from the Latin *numen*, meaning "a nod" as an expression of will. The emphasis on the will underscores the action of a personality with power, not an impersonal system of morality. The word *numen* came to signify the divine will, while the noun, *numina*, could express the might of a deity or divinity itself as a personal force. Holiness as the numinous is a charismatic force of a wholly different quality than any power in the profane world of humans. But its distinctiveness from the profane world cannot be captured by describing it either as a transcendent power in heaven or as a system of moral goodness. Instead, the numinous is a dynamic force within and beneath the profane world, where it resides as a raw and personal power beyond the boundaries of any moral system. Otto sought to capture the character of holiness by describing it as pre-moral and ineffable, by which he meant both indescribable and overwhelming. The numinous is an "over-plus of meaning," which can be neither contained with any concepts, such as goodness or beauty, nor reduced to a more fundamental state.

Thus, holiness for Otto, as the wholly other, is an immanent power within (or, perhaps better, beneath) the profane world, which exists prior to any moral system. It is not the content of religion, since the content of religion is already controlled by human concepts of morality and goodness. Rather, holiness is the "void" or "emptiness." It is the pre-moral matrix, which is the subject matter of religion. The unprovoked attack of God in Exodus 4:22–26, when Yahweh arbitrarily sought to kill Moses during the night, captures the dynamic and pre-moral quality of the numinous for Otto. Scholars struggle in vain to provide moral content to the story, seeking a cause for the arbitrary nature of the divine assault. Such a search is wrongheaded, according to Otto, since the episode probes the pre-moral character of the numinous. Otto quotes Goethe's *Faust* (part 2, act 1, scene 5) to describe the experience of such power as a deeply felt monster (*Ungeheuer*).[17]

THE SACRED AND THE PROFANE. The sacred quality of the numinous is not permanently separated from the profane world of humans. The numinous is a spiritual reality, which can be appropriated through religious feeling as it invades a human. Humans cannot control the invasion of the numinous. A person cannot prepare for the religious feeling that results from an encounter with the numinous, nor can such an encounter be restricted to the sanctuary. The numinous blows where it will, and the religious feeling that results from its invasion is neither rational thought nor psychological self-evaluation. Rational reflection on morality may clarify aspects of one's religious beliefs, but it is not able to penetrate the pre-moral numinous. The same is true with feelings of dependency or personal insufficiency. These categories are too psychological to probe the numinous at the core of religious experience. Both rational reflection and psychological feelings of dependency are controlled by the human ego. Religious feeling, according to Otto, is "creature-consciousness," which empties the ego upon the direct and present experience of the *numen*.[18] Humans who are invaded by the numinous are undone by its power, lacking even the language to describe the experience. Many of my students at seminary recall the experience of the numinous as the point of origin for their quest for ordination. The experience of the numinous in this case inaugurates the phase of separation in their rite of passage toward ordination. The quest for the proper language to describe the encounter becomes one of the goals of their seminary education.

The transfer of the numinous to humans is charismatic in nature. The word charismatic derives from the Greek *charisma*, meaning "favor" or "gift." The gift of the numinous is a direct, immediate, and personal invasion. The numinous cannot be taught, nor can it be transmitted through ritual processes restricted to sacred locations. Rather, the immediacy of the numinous presses upon humans, creating a sense of urgency that lacks specific content. Thus, humans cannot grasp holiness; they can only receive it as a spiritual gift—a *charisma*. The direct transmission of holiness is an awakening, according to Otto, of an inborn capacity to receive its essential nature. Teaching and ritual may enhance the awe of the worshiper, but they are not themselves "really spiritual." Theory, dogma, exhortation, and ritual cannot replace the essential charismatic nature of the direct transmission of holiness through the inspiration of personal feeling, expressed in the words *mysterium, tremendum*, and fascination. Those who lack this experience are encouraged by Otto to cease their quest for holiness.

THE SACRED AND ORDINATION. A sacred person or a religious leader, according to Otto, is someone who has experienced the invasion of the numinous and knows the quality of the religious experience. Otto writes:

> The reader is invited to direct his mind to a moment of deeply-felt religious experience, as little as possible qualified by other forms of consciousness. Whoever cannot do this, whoever knows no such moments in his experience, is requested to read no farther; for it is not easy to discuss questions of religious psychology with one who can recollect the emotions of his adolescence, the discomforts of indigestion, or, say, social feeling, but cannot recall any intrinsically religious feelings.[19]

This quotation underscores that, when holiness is conceived as the dynamic force of the numinous, a human cannot be trained to receive it. Expertise in the ritual practices of the sanctuary, the distribution of sacraments, and training in morality will not penetrate to the charismatic power of the *numen*. Nor can holiness be restricted to a professional class of the ordained. Any human is potentially open to the invasion of the numinous.

A holy person is someone who has been invaded directly by the numinous and knows the core experience of religious feeling with its sense of dread, awe, fear, and fascination. The passive reception of the numinous through religious feeling and the loss of the ego through the experience of the void are charismatic gifts, which are the necessary prerequisites for the proper construction of morality and religious practice. The ideal model of such a holy person is a prophet, not a priest. Otto writes: "The capital instance of the intimate mutual interpenetration of the numinous with the rational and moral is Isaiah."[20] The prophet Isaiah's reception of the numinous is immediate and personal, and his moral vision springs directly from his religious feeling. Thus, the ethical demands of Isaiah, and the prophets in general, provide the content and the consummation of the numinous. Max Weber's discussion of charismatic leadership clarifies further the results of the infusion of the numinous into a person. The infusion of charisma becomes evident, according to Weber, in the quality of an individual personality, which sets a person apart as one endowed with exceptional powers and qualities for authoritative leadership.[21] Such power is first and foremost personal, rather than institutional.

The work of Rudolf Otto on the numinous underscores the close relationship between the charismatic understanding of holiness as a dynamic force and an interpretation of ordination as the power of the prophetic word, which is potentially available to all persons. Holiness, conceived as the numinous, will provide the background for interpreting the ordination to the word in the book of Deuteronomy and in the New Testament.

Jacob Milgrom and Holiness as a Ritual Resource

THE SEPARATE QUALITY OF HOLINESS. The insights of Otto loom in the background of Milgrom's study of holiness. The separate character of the holy is important to his work, as it is for Otto. Milgrom even notes that the root meaning of holiness in Hebrew is likely the "numinous, irrational, and ineffable aspects of the deity."[22] Thus, Milgrom would agree with Otto that holiness is a dynamic power, which cannot be reduced to moral systems of behavior. But Milgrom departs from Otto's interpretation of holiness as a charismatic force in order to explore more carefully the spatial separation of holiness, as a sacred ritual resource that is distinct from the profane world. The shift in focus highlights, for Milgrom, the importance of sacred space, rather than the category of religious experience, which is so central to Otto. The shift also means that the key for interpreting the quality of holiness for Milgrom will become the cultic rituals performed in the sacred space of the sanctuary, rather than the charisma of religious feeling.

Milgrom concludes that holiness is not a primal matrix nor an "overplus of meaning" that is available directly to all humans through religious feeling. The separate quality of holiness is, rather, a spatial reality. Holiness is the realm of God in distinction from the world of humans. Holiness, therefore, is "that which is withdrawn from common use," be it a place or precinct, an object or person.[23] The emphasis on the spatial character of holiness leads to the central role of sanctuaries as the location where holiness invades the world, in contrast to the more charismatic role, in the work of Otto, of the numinous, which is able to seize humans directly and immediately in any location.[24]

The more restrictive role of holiness within sanctuaries does not lessen its dynamic power. Holiness is continually active and forceful. Holiness may enter the world through the sacred location of a sanctuary, but it seeks to transfer its power to the impure and profane world in order to lay claim to all of creation. Holiness as a ritual resource, therefore, is not simply in service to the sanctuary. Rather, it is compelled to combat the impurity that has taken over the profane world, since the root power of holiness is divinely created life itself. As a result, the sanctuary and its rituals become an ethical resource for healing and transforming the violence of the profane and impure world.[25]

Impurity is the obstacle to holiness in achieving the goal of a transformed world. The resistance of impurity occurs in two ways. First, impurity is incompatible with holiness, which means that the two forces cannot occupy the same space. Radiation poisoning again provides an example. Radiation cannot share the same space with pure air and water; one must drive the other away. Thus, when holiness seeks to transfer its healing power from the sacred space of the sanctuary to the profane world, it can be restrained in fulfilling its goal by physical and moral impurity. Death and disease cannot share the same space with the life-giving power of holiness. Ethical impurity in humans, such as violence, also has the power to resist holiness, adding further to the environmental pollution of the profane world.

Second, impurity, like holiness, is an active and dynamic force in the world. Humans, who embody the impurity of violence, can pollute sacred space and, in so doing, drive holiness from the sanctuary. The merging of God and country into a national or civil religion is a further example of the dynamic power of impurity to invade the sanctuary and to drive away holiness. These examples illustrate that impurity is not merely an obstacle to holiness as it seeks to purify the profane world; it is also a threat to the sanctuary and the very presence of holiness on earth. As a result, holiness in the sanctuary must be rigorously protected from the impurity of the profane world through clear separation. Impure persons must be purged through rituals, and the nation-state cannot be allowed to take possession of the sanctuary. God and country cannot occupy the same space by using the rituals of the sanctuary to support a civil religion.

The competing forces of holiness and impurity create a volatile and dangerous relationship between the sacred space of the sanctuary and the impurity of the profane world. The danger is expressed primarily with regard to the sanctuary, since it must be protected at all times from the contamination of impurity, if humans are to have a ritual resource of holiness. The danger of contamination to the sacred space of the sanctuary provides the primary definition of holiness for Milgrom as "that which is unapproachable except through divinely imposed restrictions."[26]

THE SACRED AND THE PROFANE. Rudolf Otto's charismatic interpretation of holiness as a dynamic power focused on the relationship between God and humans. The transfer of holiness to the profane world is a direct invasion of the numinous into humans. As a result, the sacred space of the sanctuary was not a primary focus in the work of Otto. But the sanctuary assumes a central role in the spatial interpretation of holiness. The transfer of holiness into the profane realm creates a separate environment from the impure world of humans, which is concentrated in the physical space of the sanctuary. It does not invade humans directly. Instead, holiness invades a location, creating a sacred place. A contemporary example of the spatial view of holiness is the "sanctuary movement," in which churches in the southwestern United States declare their buildings to be a distinct realm from the state and thus immune from political laws regarding migrants. Holiness, moreover, does not merely fill the space of the sanctuary, it actually adheres to objects within the sanctuary.[27] This is a sacramental view of holiness in which the water of baptism and the bread and wine of the Eucharist become infused with holiness and take on power to transform humans who come into contact with them.

Holiness remains dangerous to humans when it is understood as a ritual resource, as is the case with the numinous in the interpretation of Otto. But this danger of holiness must be stated differently. Otto underscored the danger of the numinous by exploring the overpowering nature of religious feeling and the loss of ego that occurs when holiness invades a person, creating awareness of creature-consciousness with the accompanying feelings of dread and awe. The transfer of holiness as a ritual resource is not the spiritual charisma envisioned by Otto, available directly to humans through religious feeling. In this instance, holiness is not an awakening at all, since it is never transferred charismatically to humans. Instead, the invasion of holiness into the profane world creates a separate environment within the physical space of the sanctuary, apart from the impure world of humans. In this view of holiness, churches become sanctuaries or places of refuge from the profane world and resources for health.

The spatial interpretation of holiness requires a different formulation of its danger to humans, as trespass into the sacred. Milgrom states that the danger of holiness is its ability to "cause death to the unwary and the impure who approach [it] without regard for the regulations that govern [its] usage."[28] The apostle Paul illustrates the ritual danger of holiness when he warns that the Eucharist may be an occasion of judgment, rather than blessing, to the participant who does not undertake careful self-examination (1 Cor 11:27–33). The story of the golden calf in Exodus 32, with its monarchical associations to King Jeroboam in 1 Kings 12, illustrates the deadly consequences of confusing the profane world of the king with the sacred realm of the sanctuary, when God states to Moses, concerning the fate of the Israelites who built the calf: "Now let me alone, so that my wrath may burn hot against them and I may consume them" (Ex 32:10).

Once the influence of holiness is concentrated in the sanctuary, sacred rituals rather than the charismatic power of the numinous become the means by which holiness is transferred to humans. The means of transfer are the ritual procedures, which bring the worshiper into physical contact with holiness. Holiness as a ritual resource is a dynamic force within the sanctuary. It has the power to heal worshipers from the contamination of impurity and, at the same time, to empower them to be ethical agents of holiness in the profane world. Thus, holiness as sacred space can protect as a place of asylum. Such a view of holiness and its transfer through the washing with water or the eating of bread and wine is decidedly noncharismatic.

THE SACRED AND ORDINATION. When holiness is interpreted as a ritual resource, the identity of sacred persons and the office of ordination are associated with the role of the priest. The holy status of a priest is not the immediate and personal invasion of the numinous, as is the case in Otto's view. Rather, candidates for the priesthood undergo training in order to achieve standards necessary to become ritual celebrants in the sacred space of the sanctuary.[29] The ordination of the priest demands a carefully orchestrated rite of passage, which begins with rituals of cleansing before it proceeds to sanctification.[30]

The ritual of ordination for the priest centers on the process of clothing, in conjunction with washing and anointing. The transfer of holiness through clothing provides a stark contrast to the dynamic invasion of the numinous through religious feeling. Yet it is the investiture of a person with priestly clothing that is at the heart of the ritual of consecration. Milgrom notes the importance of clothing with the following rabbinical quotation: "When the priests are clothed in their vestments, their priesthood is upon them; when they are not clothed in their vestments, their priesthood is not upon them."[31] The vestments enable the priests to mediate the power of holiness through ritual practices. The clothing transfers holiness to the priest, while it also protects the priest from the danger of holiness, much like their gear protects firefighters. We might also view the priestly vestments as masking the personality of the priest, thus providing an even sharper contrast to the emphasis on the person of the prophet in the interpretation of Otto.

The work of Jacob Milgrom underscores the close relationship between holiness as a ritual resource and ordination as the power of the priest to mediate sacramental rituals in the sanctuary. Holiness as a ritual resource will provide the background for interpreting the ordination to sacramental rituals in the priestly literature and in the New Testament.

Conclusion

Holiness, whose root meaning is separation, is an essential characteristic of God. We have seen that interpreters explore the nature of the separation of holiness in many different ways. Mircea Eliade speaks of the two modes of experience to separate the sacred and the profane. Rudolf Otto describes holiness as the wholly other, which resides as a raw power beneath the profane world. Jacob Milgrom uses more spatially oriented imagery for holiness as "that which is withdrawn from the common." The point of agreement in the different conceptions of holiness is separation, which is meant to underscore that holiness is not a power of our world, nor is it of our making. Holiness derives from God, and we can only acquire it through an action of God, which occurs either as a direct invasion into the deepest resources of a person or as a ritual that is carefully dispensed in the sanctuary. In both cases, holiness is dangerous to humans, yet it is also crucial to human life and health.

Ordination for ministry allows for the safe transfer of the sacred to the profane world of humans. The ordained must undergo a rite of passage to achieve the liminal status of those who are able to bridge the gap between the sacred and the profane. The twofold structure of ordination to word and sacrament in Christian tradition derives from the dual character of holiness. We have seen that ordination to word and sacrament is rooted in the two methods by which God invades our profane world. On one hand, holiness is a charismatic force, which is aimed more narrowly at the person and is mediated directly through religious feeling. The power of charismatic holiness is in the relationship between God and the one who is called out. The special relationship is evident in the prophetic word of the ordained, where the human ego becomes transparent, allowing God to speak through a person. On the other hand, holiness is also a ritual resource, which invades the sanctuary and resides in sacraments. The power of holiness is not in the relationship between God and the ordained. It is, rather, in the status of the ordained person, which allows him or her to come into close proximity to sacred objects. This characteristic of holiness is decidedly noncharismatic, since it is transmitted to humans through carefully constructed ritual practices, administered by priests who must wear the proper clothing.

The dual character of holiness is a central topic of theological reflection in the formation of the Torah. Both dimensions of holiness shape the life story of Moses in Torah. The book of Deuteronomy emphasizes the more charismatic quality of holiness in advocating a theology of the word in its presentation of Moses, while the priestly literature in Exodus 19 through Numbers 10 explores in more detail the way in which holiness becomes a ritual resource for the people of God when Moses assumes the role of priest. Thus, it is not surprising that each body of literature advocates a different view of ordination in its idealization of Moses. Deuteronomy idealizes Moses as the charismatic teacher of scripture who is able to persuade the Israelites to follow God, while the priestly literature describes Moses as the mediator of sacramental rituals. Both traditions influence the formation of the New Testament. The dynamic relationship between the dual characteristics of holiness and ordination can be seen in figure 2.2.

In the following chapters, we will investigate the biblical guidelines for constructing a contemporary understanding of ordination to word and sacrament. The central texts will be the book of Deuteronomy and

The Sacred	
Holiness as a Dynamic Force	*Holiness as a Ritual Resource*
The Mosaic Office	
Ordination to the Divine Word	*Ordination to Sacramental Rituals l*

FIGURE 2.2

the priestly literature, as well as their influence in the New Testament. In chapter 3, we will explore the important role of Moses in the Torah as providing the paradigm for ordination to the divine word and sacramental rituals. In chapter 4, we will explore the ordination to the divine word in the book of Deuteronomy, before turning to the ordination to sacramental rituals in the priestly literature of Exodus 19 through Numbers 10 in chapter 5. The chapters will follow in general the three-part division from our interpretation of Rudolf Otto and Jacob Milgrom: (1) the separate quality of holiness; (2) the sacred and the profane; and (3) the sacred and ordination.

RESOURCES FOR FURTHER STUDY

Barton, S. C. (ed.). *Holiness Past and Present*. London: Clark, 2003.

Eliade, M. *The Sacred and the Profane: The Nature of Religion*. New York: Harcourt, 1957.

Gammie, J. *Holiness in Israel*. Minneapolis, Minn.: Augsburg Fortress, 1989.

Gennep, A. van. *The Rites of Passage*. Translated from the 1908 edition by Monika B. Vizedom and Gabrielle L. Caffee. Chicago: University of Chicago Press, 1960.

Milgrom, J. *Leviticus 1–16: A New Translation with Introduction and Commentary*. AB 3A. Garden City, N.Y.: Doubleday, 1991.

———. *Leviticus 17–22: A New Translation with Introduction and Commentary*. AB 3A. Garden City, N.Y.: Doubleday, 2000.

———. *Leviticus 23–27: A New Translation with Introduction and Commentary*. AB 3B. Garden City, N.Y.: Doubleday, 2001.

Otto, R. *The Idea of the Holy: An Inquiry into the Non-Rational Factor in the Idea of the Divine and Its Relation to the Rational*, 2nd ed. Translated by John W. Harvey. Oxford: Oxford University Press, 1917.

Turner, V. *The Ritual Process: Structure and Anti-Structure*. New York: Aldine de Gruyter, 1969.

Turner, V., and E. Turner. *Image and Pilgrimage in Christian Culture: Anthropological Perspectives*. New York: Columbia University Press, 1978.

Weber, M. *On Charisma and Institution Building*. Edited by S. N. Eisenstadt. Chicago: University of Chicago Press, 1968.

CHAPTER THREE

The Mosaic Office as the Model for Ordination

Biblical authors use the story of Moses to fashion a theology of ordination. Thus, the presentation of Moses in Torah will be the central focus of our study of ordination in the following three chapters. Our aim in this chapter is to understand the role of Moses in Torah as personifying the authority of ordination, which we are calling the Mosaic office. Our interpretation will be separated into three sections. First, "The Mosaic Office in Torah" will explore the corporate nature of the story of Moses as a model for ordination in ancient Israel. Second, "The Mosaic Office as a Rite of Passage" will describe the character of religious leadership in Torah, contrasting the leadership of the ordained to the heroic idealization of kings in the ancient world. Third, "The Call to the Mosaic Office and the Two Theories of Holiness" will probe the nature of religious experience in the process of discerning a call to ordination.

The Mosaic Office in Torah

The Torah recounts the invasion of the sacred into the profane world. Yahweh is the central character in the story. The book of Genesis begins with an account of divine creation, demarcating the separation between the sacred world of heaven and the profane life on earth, before narrowing in scope to trace the family stories of the ancestors. Yahweh is actively involved in the life of the ancestors in the book of Genesis, calling Abraham from Ur, wrestling with Jacob, and watching over Joseph (from a distance) in the land of Egypt. Yet the appearance of

Yahweh remains unpredictable, often occurring in visions without prior notice or accompanying rituals. God appears abruptly to Abraham in visions (Gn 15, 17), under sacred trees (Gn 18), or simply as a voice from heaven (Gn 22). God addresses Hagar in the wilderness as a messenger (Gn 16) and attacks Jacob during the night (Gn 32), before retreating from direct involvement in human affairs throughout the story of Joseph. Samuel Terrien characterizes the unpredictable appearances of Yahweh to the ancestors as "epiphanic visitations," which he likens to "the sudden encounter of two strangers who were going their separate ways."[1]

The invasion of the sacred into the profane world remains the organizing goal of the exodus from Egypt and the wilderness journey of the Israelite people, as Yahweh seeks to liberate the Israelites from slavery for worship in the wilderness. The story of the exodus completes the narration of the Pentateuch, spanning the books of Exodus, Numbers, Leviticus, and Deuteronomy. Once again, Yahweh remains the central character. The exodus begins with the absence of Yahweh in the life of Israel during the people's slave labor in Egypt. The retreat of God from human affairs underscores the separation of the sacred and the profane at the outset of the story. The division of the sacred and the profane is further accentuated through the lack of the knowledge of Yahweh by all humans in the opening chapters of the book of Exodus. The author underscores that many years have transpired since the sporadic appearances of Yahweh to the ancestors, with the result that neither the Israelites nor the Egyptians remember Yahweh (Ex 1:6–8). The separation between the sacred and the profane lays the foundation for the central themes of the exodus, including the need for the revelation of Yahweh to Israel and to the Egyptians, the description of how Yahweh will take up residency on earth in a wilderness sanctuary, the selection of an ordained group to serve Yahweh, and the rituals which will allow the Israelites to approach God regularly in a safe manner.

Moses replaces the ancestors as the central human character in the story of the exodus and the wilderness journey. His biography spans the books of Exodus, Leviticus, Numbers, and Deuteronomy, thus providing a human counterpart to the divine story of salvation history. He is born in Egypt (Ex 2), and he dies on Mount Nebo at the conclusion of the wilderness journey (Dt 34). The parallel stories of Yahweh and Moses intersect throughout the Torah, creating interdependence between divine salvation and the leadership of Moses. Moses is the first to encounter God on the divine mountain (Ex 3). He is commissioned to speak to

Pharaoh for Yahweh (Ex 3–6), to lead the Israelites out of Egypt (Ex 13–14), to convey the divine word to the people at Mount Sinai (Ex 19–21) and at Mount Horeb (Dt 4–5), to mediate the covenant between Yahweh and Israel (Ex 21–24; Deuteronomy), to build a sanctuary for Yahweh in the wilderness (Ex 25–40), to instruct the Israelites in cultic rituals (Leviticus), and to guide the people to the land of promise (Numbers). Thus, salvation history and the life story of Moses progress together throughout the Torah in an organic manner, in contrast to the sporadic and random appearances of Yahweh to the ancestors.

The result of the constant interweaving of salvation history and the life of Moses is that his story is far more than a biography which traces the exploits of a hero. S. Dean McBride suggests that the life of Moses is more transcendent than that of a popular hero. His life story is bound up with a larger divine drama. For McBride, this means that when Moses acts, he acts for God. And when Moses speaks, he speaks for God.[2] The divine drama and the life of Moses could not be further removed from the epiphanic visitations of Yahweh to the ancestors, where revelation was likened to "the sudden encounter of two strangers . . . going their separate ways." God is the constant hero in the life of Moses, with the result that his story cannot be limited to an individual biography or to occasional encounters with Yahweh. Instead, Moses is part of the story of salvation history itself, since he provides a crucial and constant lifeline between Yahweh and Israel. In this role, Moses becomes a corporate character who mediates divine authority into the religious institutions of law and cultic ritual in ancient Israel.

Brevard Childs introduced the term *Mosaic office* to capture the corporate nature of the story of Moses as a paradigm for religious authority.[3] The Mosaic office in Torah models the office of ministry in ancient Israel, according to Childs, which allows for institutionalized ways of communicating with God. Thus, when Moses builds temples, hears the voice of God, speaks for Yahweh, mediates the covenant, writes law, performs sacramental rituals, heals people, and judges disputes, the biblical authors are exploring the nature of ordination in ancient Israel. When Moses mediates revelation at Mount Sinai and is authenticated as the leader of the people, the aim of the biblical author is to institutionalize the office of covenant mediator beyond the biography of Moses and into the ongoing worship life of Israel. Childs concludes that the portrayal of Moses as the mediator of covenant must be interpreted institutionally as part of the Mosaic office of ordination in Torah.

In this way, the origins of all religious authority, law, and cultic ritual are embedded in the story of Moses, which is intended to provide the resources for a biblical theology of ordination.[4] Our interpretation of ordination in the Hebrew Bible and in the New Testament will be grounded in the life story of Moses.

The Mosaic office influences the composition of the Torah. The story of Moses is often fashioned to clarify two contrasting offices of ordination, one prophetic and charismatic in nature and the other priestly and ritualistic. Thus, as noted by Brevard Childs, "the portrayal of Moses moves in different directions, depending on what office of ordination is highlighted."[5] Consequently, biblical writers often present two stories of the same event in the Torah to accentuate the prophetic and the priestly dimensions of the Mosaic office. Moses receives two calls to ordination; one is prophetic in character (Ex 3–4) and the other is priestly (Ex 6–7). There are also two accounts of Moses receiving revelation at the divine mountain, one as a charismatic teacher at Mount Horeb (Dt 4–5) and the other as a priest at Mount Sinai (Ex 19–40). The distinctive accounts of revelation provide insight into the larger design of Torah, in which the prophetic ordination of Moses is developed in the book of Deuteronomy and his priestly role in the book of Leviticus. Even the passing on of the Mosaic office requires two accounts. The prophetic office of Moses is passed on charismatically in Numbers 11 and again in Deuteronomy 31, when his spirit invades the elders of Israel and Joshua in the tent of meeting. The role of Moses as priest, by contrast, is transmitted to Aaron and his sons in Leviticus 8–9 through the performance of rituals accompanied by physical touch in the Tabernacle. The following section will explore the ordination of Moses as a rite of passage, before examining the distinctive call experiences to the prophetic and priestly offices.

The Mosaic Office as a Rite of Passage

The story of Moses is structured into a rite of passage.[6] The narrative of Moses's birth, flight from Egypt, encounter with Yahweh in the wilderness, and eventual return to Egypt as the leader of the Israelite people conforms to the structure of the rite of passage, described in chapter 2. The rite of passage culminates in the permanent transformation of Moses as a religious leader, when his face is invaded by divine light. A brief summary of Moses's rite of passage will provide background for interpreting the theology of ordination in Torah.

The birth of Moses is important for the development of the Mosaic office. Moses is born during the Israelite slavery in Egypt at a time when Pharaoh commands all male Hebrew babies to be killed by drowning in the Nile River (Ex 1:22), because of his fear of the population growth of the Israelites. The story of Moses's birth in Exodus 2:1–10 is familiar. He is conceived in secret by a Levitical couple. When his mother can no longer hide him at three months of age, she floats him on the Nile River in a basket, placing it in the reeds at the edge of the river. Surprisingly, the daughter of Pharaoh descends to the river, discovers the baby, and adopts him as her own, thus raising the Hebrew child as an Egyptian in the palace of Pharaoh, until Moses takes on his role as the leader of the Israelite nation.

The birth story of Moses is told in the genre of the heroic legend, in which a future champion is abandoned, set adrift on water, and eventually adopted in secret, until he achieves his public office of leadership. The legend is most often applied to kings. Herodotus, for example, uses a variant of the story to describe the birth of Cyrus, the Persian king.[7] Brian Lewis has identified no less than seventy-two variations of the story, of which the most striking parallel to the birth of Moses is *The Legend of Sargon*, the tale of the famous king of Akkad from the third millennium B.C.E., who functions as the prototypical king in Mesopotamian literature. In the story, Sargon is the infant of a priestess, who is prohibited from conceiving a child. She disobeys, conceives Sargon in secret, and floats the baby on the river in a vessel of reeds. Sargon is rescued from the river and adopted by Akki, the water drawer, who raises him as a gardener, until he returns to Akkad as king.[8]

The heroic legend is based on the rite of passage, in which the hero is separated from his family and people, undergoes trial during a liminal period of transition, and returns to his family or people, having undergone transformation, which empowers leadership.[9] The genre is appropriately described by Brevard Childs as a "rags-to-riches" story, which authenticates a hero for leadership.[10] There is little doubt that the biblical author has used the heroic legend to describe the birth of Moses as a rite of passage. The parallels between *The Sargon Legend* and Moses's birth story include anonymous parents from the priestly class, an illegal birth, a river ordeal, rescue, adoption, and the return of the hero to his people.

The literary context of the story of Moses's birth also departs from the heroic legend to provide a contrast between the rite of passage of the traditional hero and the ideal religious leader in the biblical tradition. In the traditional form of the legend, the rite of passage of the hero begins with a separation from family, followed by a liminal period of testing and the threat of death, which transforms the hero from a position of anonymity to public leadership. The biblical writers employ the legend in order to reject the heroic ideal in the birth story of Moses. Moses certainly undergoes the heroic rite of passage and he is, indeed, exalted into the family of Pharaoh. But his exaltation is only momentary, since he quickly returns to the status of a hunted slave, when Pharaoh seeks his life (Ex 2:15). Many interpret the inverted structure against the backdrop of the Israelites' slavery and the need for Moses to become a savior of slaves, which is, indeed, true.[11] If this were the primary reason for the reshaping of Moses's birth story, the account would still conform to the heroic legend, only adapting the genre to the social setting of slavery. The additional changes to the birth story of Moses indicate, however, that the biblical author rejects the heroic legend altogether as the appropriate rite of passage for religious leadership.

The biblical author's rejection of the heroic rite of passage is made evident in the first action of Moses as an adult in Exodus 2:11–15. In the heroic pattern, Moses should return to his people as a transformed and successful leader. Exodus 2:11–15 lays the groundwork for such a story, when Moses is described as returning to the Hebrews as an adult, who opposes the slave status of the Israelites. Moses reacts by killing an Egyptian as an act of liberation, thus fulfilling the heroic genre (Ex 2:12). The biblical author rejects the heroic rite of passage, however, by turning the story into an illustration of failed leadership, when a Hebrew identifies the action of Moses as nothing more than murder, performed in secret (Ex 2:13–14). The public proclamation of Moses's secret act of murder transforms him into an antihero, who flees from his people to save his own life (Ex 2:15). The story of Moses's murder of the Egyptian and flight from Egypt indicates that the biblical author rejects the heroic legend as the ideal rite of passage for religious leadership. The fulfillment of the Mosaic office of ordination will require a different rite of passage than that of the traditional hero.

The biblical author overlays the heroic legend of Moses's birth with an additional rite of passage, which is intended to probe the nature of ordination to the Mosaic office. The rite of passage of ordination begins with Moses's flight from his people as a failed hero. Thus, the loss of self-determination and self-sufficiency becomes an important factor in the process of ordination to the Mosaic office. The ritual of separation suggests a breakdown of the human ego, which opens Moses to the potential for new experiences beyond the boundaries of his own self-will and sense of power. The ritual of separation in the rite of passage is indicated geographically in the journey of Moses from Egypt into the wilderness. Victor Turner notes that the wilderness often indicates the liminal stage in a rite of passage, as a location on the threshold of organized society and human experience, where a person undergoes trials and testing.[12] The wilderness trials of Jesus in the gospel tradition come immediately to mind (Mk 1:12–13; Mt 4:1–11; Lk 4:1–13). The tradition of Jesus' rite of passage in the wilderness is actually based on the story of Moses, who comes to symbolize the pattern in biblical tradition in which a religious leader goes through a rite of passage in the wilderness.

Moses undergoes a series of experiences in the wilderness, which bring about his transformation from a failed hero to the religious leader of the Israelites. He initially enters the Midianite family of Jethro, marries Zipporah, and has a son, Gershom (Ex 2:15–22). In naming his son, Moses describes the transformation of his identity from the self-sufficient hero to the more vulnerable status of a resident alien: "I have been an alien residing in a foreign land" (Ex 2:22). The wilderness transformation of Moses continues with his new occupation as a shepherd, in place of his previous status as a prince. Moses's role as shepherd eventually brings him to the divine mountain, where he encounters Yahweh for the first time, receives a commission, and is given signs of sacred power from God to authenticate his role as a religious leader. The wilderness trials of Moses continue with further struggles, including a divine attack (Ex 4:24–26), until he returns to Egypt transformed as a religious leader, who publicly represents Yahweh's claim on the Israelites to Pharaoh regardless of the consequences (Ex 5).[13]

The literary design of the story of Moses indicates that the biblical author employs the heroic legend in the birth story of Moses in a critical way. The rite of passage of the hero leads to failure in the story of Moses. The success of Moses resides in a new rite of passage, which characterizes the religious leadership of the Mosaic office. In the new paradigm, the act of separation not only includes the physical removal of Moses from his people, but also his loss of self-sufficiency. The new sense of vulnerability, as a resident alien in a foreign land, leads to a transformative encounter with Yahweh in the liminal setting of the wilderness. In the opening story of Moses as a prince in Egypt, he sought to save his people through violence, even while he feared for his life. After his encounter with Yahweh, Moses returns to Egypt to confront Pharaoh and to demand the liberation of the Hebrew slaves, not as a hero, but as the messenger of Yahweh.

The rite of passage of Moses as a religious leader differs in yet another way from the heroic legend. In the heroic legend, the king is separated from the people in order to undergo transformation. Yet he also reenters the profane world of the nation in order to lead the people. Unlike the heroic king, Moses is never completely reintegrated into the profane social world of the Israelites. The rite of passage of ordination means that Moses remains in a constant liminal state, even when he returns to lead the Israelites out of Egypt and into the wilderness. Thus, Moses never becomes a king. Instead, his sacred authority remains distinct from the power of the profane state. Victor Turner provides insight into the rite of passage of Moses, when he notes that liminality can become a permanent institutionalized state, especially in rites of passage associated with the sacred and ordination.

The liminal status of the Mosaic office is a result of its sacred character, which is indicated most clearly in the story of Moses's shining face (Ex 34:29–35).[14] The events leading up to this episode in the book of Exodus provide background for interpreting the nature of ordination to the Mosaic office. Once Moses undergoes the rite of passage of a religious leader (Ex 1–7), he successfully represents Yahweh to Pharaoh during the events of the exodus (Ex 8–14), which is followed by his leading the Israelites into the wilderness on a journey to the divine mountain (Ex 15–18). Biblical writers use the setting of the wilderness to explore the role of Moses as a religious leader, who mediates between Yahweh and the Israelite people, just as they use this setting to explore Moses's call to ordination (Ex 3–7). The role of Moses as mediator is greatly expanded during the revelation of the law (Ex 19–34). Through repeated trips to the summit of the mountain, Moses begins to model the offices of priest, prophetic teacher, and even scribe as he purifies Israel, teaches the people the covenant, and records divine law. The portrayal of Moses as a religious leader culminates in his final descent from the divine mountain in Exodus 34:29–35, when his face is permanently invaded by divine light, indicating his transformation to the Mosaic office of ordination.

Exodus 34:29–35 recounts the descent of Moses from Mount Sinai with the two tablets of the covenant, signifying his ability to mediate between the sacred and the profane. The episode divides between a description of Moses's transformation, in which his face is invaded by divine light (Ex 34:29–32), and its implications for Moses's interaction with the Israelite people, where he is separated from them with a veil (Ex 34:33–35). The divine light and the veil probe the divine authority of the Mosaic office and the relationship of the sacred and the profane for the ordained. Three aspects of ordination emerge from the story.

First, the motif of divine light underscores the divine origin of ordination and the liminal status of the Mosaic office. The shining skin of Moses signifies his transfer from the profane world of humans to the sacred realm of God. The transformation of Moses is underscored further when the biblical author notes that Aaron and the other leaders of Israel fear him: "When Aaron and all the Israelites saw Moses, the skin of his face was shining, and they were afraid to come near him" (Ex 34:30).

Second, ordination is a divine action, not a human decision. Moses is unaware of his changed status: "Moses did not know that the skin of his face shone because he had been talking with God" (Ex 34:29). The ignorance of Moses about his transformation is meant to clarify that his own charisma cannot account for the authority of the Mosaic office. Thus, even though the speech of Yahweh and Moses merge into one voice at the divine mountain, the power of the Mosaic office does not arise from the profane character of Moses, but rests with the deity.

Third, the Mosaic office places the ordained in a permanent liminal state. The divine light never leaves the face of Moses, in spite of the apostle Paul's interpretation to the contrary in 2 Corinthians 3:12–18. The permanent transformation of Moses's face forces him to wear a veil outside of the cult: "When Moses had finished speaking with them [the Israelites], he put a veil on his face" (Ex 34:33). The veil indicates that even when Moses leaves the setting of the sacred and enters the profane world, he remains separate from the people. The result is that Moses is permanently set apart from the Israelite people through his ordination to the Mosaic office. The shining face separates Moses from the people in the setting of worship, and the veil sets him apart from the profane world outside of the sanctuary.

The characteristics of the Mosaic office as the model for ordination are now clearly in view. The rite of passage to the Mosaic office is firmly anchored in the world of the sacred. The separation of the sacred and the profane is indicated in the biblical author's rejection of the heroic legend, in which a future king undergoes transformation to become a political leader. The ritual of separation for Moses departs from the heroic legend. His separation includes an anonymous childhood apart from his family, but it also includes the breakdown of his ego, which opens him to the potential for new experiences beyond the boundaries of his own sense of power. The biblical author extends the separation of the sacred and the profane further in the story of the shining face of Moses. The divine light invades Moses permanently, requiring that he wear a veil at all times in the profane world. The veil ensures Moses's separation from the profane world with its distinct forms of political leadership.

The restriction of the Mosaic office to the service of the sacred is indicated most clearly in Exodus 32 in the story of the golden calf, which is a political allegory about the desire to merge the sacred and the profane into a theological interpretation of the king or the state. The repetition of this story during the reign of King Jeroboam I in 1 Kings 12 is meant to provide the political background to the golden calf.[15] In this story, King Jeroboam I is a failed monarch, who fears for his security and desires to merge the sacred and the profane to provide religious authority in support of his rule. To this end, Jeroboam I makes two golden calves, one in Bethel and another in Dan, and proclaims: "Here are your gods, O Israel, who brought you up out of the land of Egypt" (1 Kgs 12:28). The attempt of Jeroboam I to claim the divine right to rule represents the invasion of the profane into the sacred world. This action is judged to be the sin which leads to the downfall of his kingdom (1 Kgs 13). In Exodus 32, Aaron is presented as a failed religious leader, who also gives in to the temptation to merge the sacred and the profane through the construction of a golden calf. The close literary relationship between Aaron and Jeroboam I is indicated when Aaron repeats the language of Jeroboam I by crediting the leading of the Israelites from Egypt to two calves, even though he builds only one. Aaron states: "These are your gods, O Israel, who brought you up out of the land of Egypt" (Ex 32:4).

The sin of the golden calf by Jeroboam I, the political leader, and by Aaron, the religious leader, is the same. Each character desires to merge the sacred and the profane, which pollutes the sacred and drives the deity away. Exodus 32 idealizes Moses as the religious leader who maintains the separation of the sacred and the profane by destroying the golden calf and judging it to be an idol. An idol, according to the rabbis, is a form of greed, in which profane humans desire to possess and to control the sacred power of God.[16] The Mosaic office represents the rejection of such greed.

The Call to the Mosaic Office and the Two Theories of Holiness

All persons ordained to ministry in biblical tradition require a divine call to the vocation, which must be publicly authenticated. The call is an essential feature of the rite of passage and the authentication of the call is crucial, since without it religious leaders lack vocational identity and divine authority. Biblical authors model the call to ordination within the story of Moses. The authors identify two distinct types of call experiences by Moses, which correspond to the two theories of holiness as a dynamic force and as a ritual resource. As a result, Moses's rite of passage to the Mosaic office includes a call to ordination as a prophetic leader in Exodus 3–4 and as a priest in Exodus 6–7.

The two commissions of Moses explore the distinctive experiences of holiness in the rite of passage of ordination. The prophetic call of Moses in Exodus 3–4 is grounded in a sudden and unexpected encounter, in which Yahweh invades Moses by appearing to him in the burning bush and challenging him to lead the Israelites from Egypt. The commission is introspective, probing the fears and doubts of Moses. The locale of the wilderness sets the stage for the call's liminal character and introspective focus. The authentication of the commission is charismatic. The elders of the Israelites must recognize the power of God in Moses and acquire faith in him by seeing his charismatic gifts for leadership. The priestly call of Moses in Exodus 6–7 lacks the introspection of the prophetic call. The more public focus of the call is accentuated by the setting of the land of Egypt, as compared to Moses's isolated experience in the wilderness. The identity of Moses as an authentic leader is established through genealogy and not by an act of faith in the charismatic qualities of Moses. The power of holiness is also more institutional in the priestly commission of Moses; it is a ritual resource that will bring public acts of judgment on the Egyptians and their gods.

The interpretation of the two calls of Moses will explore the distinctive experiences of the two stories, noting in particular how the call experiences to prophet and to priest are grounded in the contrasting theories of holiness as a dynamic power and as a ritual resource. Although distinct, we will also see that the two commissions of Moses function in tandem to provide identity and authority for ordination to the Mosaic office. In the conclusion to the chapter, we will describe how the story of Moses does not allow the reader to pick and choose between the prophetic and the priestly dimensions of the Mosaic office. Instead, both the prophetic and the priestly experiences of holiness inform Moses's call to ordination.

The Prophetic Call of Moses

The literary context of the prophetic call of Moses is important for our interpretation. The wilderness setting of the commission and the isolated experience of Moses have already been noted. Moses's wilderness encounter with Yahweh in Exodus 3–4 is also tied closely to the preceding events in Exodus 2. The shepherd, who is confronted by God alone on the divine mountain, is fully developed as a character. Moses has already undergone a heroic birth and adoption (Ex 2:1–10), experienced failure as a heroic savior of the Israelites (Ex 2:11–15), and married the Midianite Zipporah (Ex 2:16–22). The literary context encourages the reader to view Moses as a complex individual by the time he encounters God in the burning bush to receive the prophetic call to ordination. The fully developed characterization of Moses, along with his isolation in the wilderness, allows the biblical author to explore the more introspective experience of holiness as a dynamic force, which invades Moses and in the process also exposes his doubts and fears about leadership.

The initial experience of the prophetic call is narrated in Exodus 3:1–6. The description of Moses's encounter with the deity is similar to Rudolf Otto's portrayal of holiness as the numinous. God appears to Moses suddenly as a dynamic and personal power, calling him by name: "Moses, Moses." The eternal flame in the bush signifies that the experience is of a wholly other quality from the profane world. The otherness of the experience is reinforced when Moses lacks the words to identify the encounter: "I must turn aside and look at this great sight, and see why the bush is not burned up" (Ex 3:4). The divine warning against trespass underscores that the wonder of holiness is dangerous to humans: "Come no closer! Remove the sandals from your feet, for the place on which you are standing is holy ground" (Ex 3:5). The reaction of Moses strengthens the comparison to Otto's description of holiness as the numinous. He is caught off guard in the encounter with God; he is simply tending sheep. It is not an experience for which he has planned or prepared. And it is certainly not an experience that he could create through rituals. Instead, the sudden appearance of the holy is a personal force, which Moses can only receive as a gift. Once Moses is awakened to the nature of the confrontation, his response is one of religious feeling, which is characterized by dread and a sense of dependency, described by Otto as creature-consciousness: "And Moses hid his face, for he was afraid to look at God" (Ex 3:6).[17]

Moses's encounter with holiness in Exodus 3:1–6 also illustrates Mircea Eliade's contrast between the sacred and the profane as "two modes of being in the world," which give rise to two different qualities of experience.[18] The burning bush represents the irruption of the sacred into the life of Moses. It generates a new point of orientation for Moses to evaluate his life experiences. The remainder of the prophetic call to ordination in Exodus 3:7–4:17 explores the inner tensions within Moses, which arise from his confrontation with the sacred. The literary unit is structured as a dialogue between Moses and Yahweh, in which Moses repeatedly resists the new orientation of the sacred, requiring God to reassure him of the authenticity of his call to ordination. The dialogical structure of the prophetic call is intended to explore the strengths and weaknesses of charismatic leadership by probing the role of the human ego in the process of discerning the call to ordination. The pattern repeats throughout the prophetic literature to authenticate the call of such prophets as Isaiah, Jeremiah, and Ezekiel.[19]

The dialogue between God and Moses is unusually long. It extends through five cycles of discourse, which repeat the same pattern of divine commission, human objection, divine reassurance, and a sign to authenticate the experience. The initial commission of Moses in Exodus 3:10–12 illustrates the pattern. God commissions Moses to rescue the Israelites from Egypt: "So come, I will send you to Pharaoh to bring my people, the Israelites, out of Egypt" (Ex 3:10). Moses resists the commission by doubting his own identity, especially in light of his previously failed attempt at leadership: "Who am I that I should go to Pharaoh and bring the Israelites out of Egypt?" (Ex 3:11). The objection prompts a divine response of reassurance: "I will be with you" (Ex 3:12). The divine reassurance is not so much a guarantee of success, as a commitment of divine presence and shared risk throughout the commission. The dialogue concludes with God offering Moses a sign to confirm the authenticity of his call experience: "And this will be a sign for you that it is I who sent you: when you have brought the people out of Egypt, you shall worship God on this mountain" (Ex 3:12).

The pattern repeats four more times. In the next cycle, Moses doubts the authenticity of the divine confrontation, stating that he does not know the name of the deity: "If I come to the Israelites and say to them, 'The God of your ancestors has sent me to you,' and they ask me, 'What is his name?' what shall I say to them?" (Ex 3:13–15). Then he doubts that others will believe in his commission: "But suppose they do not believe me or listen to me, but say, 'Yahweh did not appear to you' " (Ex 4:1–9). He resists still further by probing his personal inadequacy to fulfill the commission: "I have never been eloquent" (Ex 4:10–12). And finally, he objects to the commission by simply pleading: "O my Lord, please send someone else" (Ex 4:13–17).

Erich Auerbach provides a point of departure for interpreting the extended and repetitive dialogue in the prophetic call of Moses. He has noted that the narrative style of the Hebrew Bible tends to leave the thoughts and feelings of characters unexpressed, only suggesting the interior life through silences or fragmentary speeches.[20] Moses's fragmentary speeches of resistance to the experience of the numinous allows the biblical author to probe his inner life, as the model for how one tests the authenticity of the charismatic encounter with holiness. The repeated resistance indicates that the process of discernment in the prophetic call takes place over an extended period of time, while the literary design of the objections models a progression from external concerns about the authenticity of the religious experience and the ability of Moses to persuade others of his commission to internal doubts about his personal inadequacies. The divine reassurances to the doubts of Moses throughout the dialogue underscore the interpersonal nature of the encounter, with each response penetrating deeper into his character.

The extended dialogue between Yahweh and Moses probes Moses's new sense of self-identity, which flows from his experience of holiness in the burning bush, characterized by Mircea Eliade as a new orientation and by Rudolf Otto as creature-consciousness. The awakening to creature-consciousness is crucial to authenticate the call to prophetic ordination because of the charismatic nature of the office, with its emphasis on personal power and persuasive speech. The objections of Moses trace the emptying of his ego in the rite of passage of the prophetic call to ordination. The initial resistance to the prophetic call, "Who am I?"

establishes the theme of identity to express Moses's doubt about entering the prophetic office.

The second and third objections of Moses underscore the need for public authentication of the gift of holiness in the prophetic office. Both objections underscore the role of persuasive speech in fulfilling the office by emphasizing the need for the Israelites to believe in the message. In Exodus 3:13–15, Moses is unsure of the authenticity of his own religious experience and therefore doubts his ability to be persuasive, since he is not able to identify the deity who has called him: "If... they ask me, 'What is his name?' what shall I say to them?" The statement raises the question of how the Israelites could possibly believe in Moses's commission, when he is unable to put the experience into words. The inability to give voice to a life-transforming religious experience is a common feature of the prophetic call to ordination. Yet the charismatic nature of the prophetic office requires that the experience of holiness be described so that others are able to recognize the divine call in the person of Moses. The objection of Moses in Exodus 4:1 addresses the tension between the social and the personal quality of an ineffable experience of holiness and the need to communicate the encounter to others. Moses states: "But suppose they [the elders of the Israelites] do not believe me or listen to me." The objection of Moses captures the important goal of the training for ministry in the prophetic office of the word to acquire the language which gives voice to the religious experience of the numinous.

The fourth and fifth objections move from doubts about public persuasion and authority to probe more deeply the emptying of Moses's ego through his self-perceived weaknesses. Moses does not see himself as a charismatic speaker, nor does he see this quality changing in light of his religious experience. He tells the deity that he has never been eloquent "neither in the past nor even now that you have spoken to your servant" (Ex 4:10). The progression from the fear of public rejection to personal doubts of adequacy brings Moses to the awareness of creature-consciousness, when he pleads for release from the commission: "Please send someone else" (Ex 4:13). The final statement indicates the emptying of Moses to the invasion of holiness, which signals his readiness to undertake the prophetic call to ordination.

The sequence of Moses's fragmentary speeches of resistance to the experience of the numinous has allowed the biblical author to probe Moses's inner life as the model for how one tests the authenticity of the charismatic encounter with holiness. Central to Moses's process of discernment is the rejection of the call to the prophetic office. The charismatic experience of holiness must not be embraced too eagerly or accepted without testing. The objections signal the need to evaluate critically the religious experience of holiness as the numinous in order to separate the charisma of prophetic leadership from the heroic legend, where power resides in the human ego.

The divine reassurance to Moses throughout the extended dialogue provides commentary on the nature of the charismatic power of holiness within the prophetic office. The divine revelation begins with the promise of presence: "I will be with you" (Ex 3:12). The nature of the divine presence comes into clearer focus as Moses continues to resist the call to the prophetic office of ordination, prompting the deity to reveal more clearly the nature of holiness and in the process to penetrate more deeply into Moses. Moses's religious experience of the numinous is clarified by the revelation of the divine name, Yahweh (Ex 3:13–15), which acquires a mystical meaning in the prophetic call: "I am who I am." The divine name has puzzled interpreters because of its verbal character. The verbal phrase suggests that the meaning of the divine name cannot be discerned through contemplation of the name itself, but from reflection on the actions of God in the lives of Moses and the Israelites.

Moses's fear that his call will lack the public authority to persuade the Israelites is countered by the infusion of divine signs of power and healing, which the Israelites will experience as charismatic gifts of healing that flow from his person (Ex 4:1–9). Finally, Yahweh responds to Moses's self-perceived weakness that he lacks the charismatic power of persuasive speech by revealing that all charisma, including the power of personal leadership and persuasive speech, originates from God; it does not reside innately in humans: "Who gives speech to mortals? Who makes them mute or deaf, seeing or blind? Is it not I, Yahweh?" (Ex 4:11). The final revelation that all charisma derives from God completes the process of discernment in the prophetic call to ordination, since this insight is only possible when the human ego is emptied through the religious experience of holiness as the numinous.

We have seen that the prophetic call is introspective. The biblical author accentuates the internal and individual process of discernment by placing Moses alone in the wilderness, where he is confronted unexpectedly by holiness, which propels him into a dialogue of resistance and self-examination with the deity. The introspection and the isolated setting have allowed the biblical author to distinguish the charisma of the religious leader from that of the popular hero. But it would be a mistake to interpret the isolation and introspection of the prophetic call of Moses as a story of individual leadership. The prophetic call concludes by underscoring the limitations of Moses's charisma and his need to lead with others, rather than alone.

At the conclusion of the dialogue, the deity concedes that Moses cannot fulfill the prophetic office alone, but will require the assistance of Aaron, the Levite, who possesses the charismatic quality of persuasive speech: "What of your brother Aaron the Levite? I know that he can speak fluently" (Ex 4:14). Aaron is more familiar to readers of the Hebrew Bible as the priest, who distributes holiness through rituals. But in the prophetic call of Moses, Aaron functions as a charismatic teacher, who aids Moses in persuading the Israelites of the authenticity of his religious experience at the burning bush. The concluding words of God to Moses provide a qualification of the tendency to equate charismatic, prophetic leadership with individual control: "You [Moses] shall speak to him [Aaron] and put the words in his mouth; and I will be with your mouth and with his mouth, and will teach you what you shall do" (Ex 4:15–16). The communal nature of the charismatic leadership of the Mosaic office continues throughout Torah, when seventy of the elders (Nm 11) and Joshua (Dt 31) also assume the prophetic office with Moses.

The Priestly Call of Moses

Moses undergoes a second call to ordination in Exodus 6–7, as a priest rather than as a prophet. The literary context of Moses's priestly call to ordination is important for our interpretation, since it highlights a series of contrasts to his private experience of holiness as the numinous in the burning bush. In the present literary context, the priestly call to ordination assumes Moses's earlier encounter with holiness. Moses has already undergone the introspective self-criticism of the prophetic call, while alone in the wilderness. He has also experienced further trials in the wilderness (Ex 4:24–26) and rendezvoused with Aaron (Ex 4:27–31). The two men have returned to Egypt to represent Yahweh before Pharaoh (Ex 5:1), and they have met resistance, when Pharaoh states: "Who is Yahweh that I should heed him and let Israel go? I do not know Yahweh and I will not let Israel go" (Ex 5:2). The literary context suggests that the priestly call to ordination builds on the charismatic experience of the numinous, rather than replacing it.

Unlike the isolation and introspection of the wilderness in the prophetic call, the setting of the priestly call to ordination in Exodus 6:2–7:7 is in the land of Egypt, indicating its public and institutional context. The priestly call of Moses occurs in the midst of a social and political crisis, in which Pharaoh rejects the authenticity of Moses's prophetic call by denying the very possibility of a numinous experience with Yahweh through the statement "Who is Yahweh?" The authority of Moses in this setting is no longer rooted in his charisma nor in the ability of the Israelite people to see the numinous power of holiness in his person. Instead, the internal experience of the numinous gives way to public displays of divine power and legitimacy, which are not intended to call forth a shared religious feeling in Pharaoh or even in the Israelites. Rather, Moses is commissioned to become a ritual specialist, who mediates divine wonders into the land of Egypt. The mediation of the wonders in the form of the plagues will bring the sacred into conflict with the impure and profane world of Egypt. The result will be public displays of judgment on the Egyptian gods, which will force the Egyptians and Pharaoh to acknowledge Yahweh (Ex 7:1–5).

The priestly call of Moses illustrates the conclusion of Jacob Milgrom cited in chapter 2; he has noted that although the root meaning of holiness resides in the "numinous, irrational, and ineffable aspects of the deity," a key for interpreting holiness is also its power as a ritual resource.[21] The priestly call explores the power of holiness which is mediated through rituals, rather than through the persuasive charisma of Moses. The initial commission sets the stage for a series of ritual competitions between Aaron and Moses and the Egyptian magicians throughout the cycle of the plagues, which are meant to be public displays of divine power as the sacred lays claim to the land of Egypt (Ex 7:8–13, 8:16–19, 9:8–12). The priestly ordination will reach its final confirmation when Moses and Aaron mediate divine holiness to the Israelites through the rituals of the Tabernacle (Lv 8–9).

Moses's initial experience of holiness in the priestly call to ordination is narrated in Exodus 6:2–9. The appearance of God lacks the numinous quality of the burning bush along with the experience of an awakening within Moses. Instead, God is revealed to Moses in the context of history, tradition, and liturgy. God appears to Moses with the words: "I am Yahweh. I appeared to Abraham, Isaac, and Jacob as El Shaddai, but by my name Yahweh I did not make myself known to them" (Ex 6:2). Walter Zimmerli concludes that the phrase "I am Yahweh" is a liturgical formula by which God is introduced in the corporate setting of worship.[22] Nahum Sarna adds that the liturgy assumes a prior knowledge of God on the part of the recipient, which is reinforced in Exodus 6:2 by the divine reference to the religious experience of the ancestors.[23] Thus, unlike Moses's isolated experience of holiness in the burning bush, where he was invaded by the numinous and lacked the language to describe the event, the liturgical character of Exodus 6:2 indicates that Moses's priestly call to ordination is embedded in the rituals of worship and that the content of the experience is informed by tradition.

The interpretation of the name Yahweh to Moses during his call experience reinforces the emphasis on tradition and history in the priestly call to ordination. Moses's encounter with holiness in the revelation of the name Yahweh is not beyond description as in the prophetic experience of the burning bush, nor is it even unique in the religious tradition of Israel. Rather, Yahweh's immediate reference to the ancestors anchors the call of Moses in past religious experiences. God grounds the experience of Moses in similar appearances to the ancestors Abraham, Isaac, and Jacob, where the manifestation of the deity was in the form of El Shaddai. The reference to the past emphasizes the institutional focus of the priestly call to ordination. It indicates that the authenticity of the experience of holiness for the one being called begins within the context of tradition, as opposed to the introspective focus that arises from the invasion of the numinous in the prophetic call. Even the divine motivation for the call of Moses stems from tradition. Yahweh informs Moses of divine obligations with the ancestors from the past: "I established my covenant with them" (Ex 6:4). And it is the divine memory of covenantal obligations that is now prompting God's appearance to Moses: "I remembered my covenant" (Ex 6:5). Thus, the priestly call to ordination is not a free act of God, in which the numinous invades Moses while he is alone in the wilderness. Instead, history and tradition provide the basis for Moses's religious experience of God.

The evolution of the divine name in the priestly call to ordination, from El Shaddai to Yahweh, also underscores that tradition includes change. The revelation of the divine name Yahweh is meant to indicate something new in the tradition, which provides the content to Moses's priestly call to ordination at this juncture in the life of the Israelite people. As in the prophetic call to ordination, Moses must authenticate the new revelation. Unlike the prophetic call to ordination, the process of discernment is not the introspective and self-critical evaluation of the religious experience of the numinous. Moses's confirmation of his experience of God and his call to the priestly ordination resides in tradition, rather than in his religious feeling. He must realize that Yahweh is the same God, El Shaddai, who made a covenant with the ancestors (Gn 17, 28, 35) and that his priestly call to ordination is part of the long tradition of God's involvement in the history of Israel. As a result, the formation of identity in the priestly call to ordination replaces the self-critical evaluation of the religious experience of the numinous with a critical study of religious history and tradition. The name Yahweh incorporates the past covenantal promises of El Shaddai, while at the same time providing Moses with new ritual power to counter the resistance of Pharaoh and to demonstrate the deity's claim on the Israelite people.

The appearance of Yahweh in Exodus 6:2–9 is followed by an exchange between God and Moses in Exodus 6:10–7:5, which clarifies the process of discernment and the public authentication of Moses in the priestly call to ordination. The exchange initially encourages comparison to the prophetic call, since it is organized by Moses's resistance to the commission because of his inability to speak. Twice he states: "Since I am a poor speaker, why would Pharaoh listen to me?" (Ex 6:10, 30). The motif of poor speech in the resistance of Moses to the divine commission appears to be similar to the process of critical self-reflection in the prophetic call. But upon closer reading, it becomes evident that the formation of identity in the priestly call to ordination lacks the introspection and dialogical quality of the prophetic call. The objection of Moses does not arise from his inner doubts about the charismatic quality of persuasive speech, but from his recent public experience. At the conclusion of Moses's encounter with Yahweh, the narrator states that Moses conveyed the message to Israel: "But they would not listen to Moses, because of their broken spirit and their cruel slavery" (Ex 6:9).

The public rejection of the Israelites is important to the priestly call to ordination. It indicates that the charisma of persuasive speech will not be a criterion for the public authentication of Moses in the priestly call to ordination. In fact, the motif of the Israelites acquiring faith in Moses is absent altogether. Moses is not required to be a charismatic and persuasive speaker either to Pharaoh or to the Israelites. Instead, the authentication of Moses's call will occur in public acts of judgment on the

Egyptian gods, which will bring the Egyptians (Ex 7:5) and eventually the Israelites to the knowledge of Yahweh (Ex 29:46). The ritual actions of Moses and Aaron in mediating the plagues in Egypt and the glory of Yahweh into the Tabernacle, rather than persuasive speech, are the means by which the priestly call to ordination is authenticated.

The absence of introspection in Moses's objection is reinforced by the lack of any divine reassurance about the authenticity of his religious experience. The deity does not probe the inner character of Moses at any time in the priestly call to ordination. The focus is rather on the public representation of Yahweh to Pharaoh: "Go and tell Pharaoh king of Egypt to let the Israelites go out of his land" (Ex 6:10). The objection of Moses about his inability to succeed as priest is countered by locating his call to ordination within the broad context of religious tradition through a genealogy in Exodus 6:14–25. Rather than probing the character of Moses's experience of the numinous, the genealogy emphasizes the corporate nature of the call to priesthood, placing Moses within the broad tradition of priests who preceded him (Levi) and who will follow him (Eleazar and Phinehas). The genealogy emphasizes the corporate nature of Moses's priestly call to ordination to such a strong degree that interpreters debate whether Exodus 6–7 might better be interpreted as the call of Aaron, rather than Moses. The conclusion of the genealogy in Exodus 6:26–27 goes so far as to present the priestly call of ordination as a call experience of both Moses and Aaron: "It was this same Aaron and Moses to whom Yahweh said, 'Bring the Israelites out of the land of Egypt, company by company.' "

Conclusion

We have seen that Moses emerges as the most prominent character in Torah. His life story is interwoven with the divine account of salvation history. He is born during the Israelites' slavery in Egypt, and he dies on the border of the promised land at the conclusion of the wilderness journey. The parallel stories of Yahweh and Moses intersect to such a degree in Torah that the divine salvation of Israel and the leadership of Moses become interdependent. The result is that Moses models the different ways in which the sacred is mediated into the profane world through human leadership. In this role, Moses becomes a corporate character who models the office of ordination in the Torah. Brevard Childs introduced the term the Mosaic office to capture the corporate nature of the story of Moses as the model for ordination in the Torah.

Moses acquires the role of mediator through a rite of passage, in which he is transferred from the profane world to the sacred realm. We saw that the rite of passage of the religious leader contrasts to the traditional heroic model of leadership. The birth story of Moses critically evaluates the heroic legend, in which a future king undergoes a ritual of separation from his family before assuming the role of the ideal political leader. The political model of leadership in the heroic legend does not probe the sacred origin of the power of the ordained. Thus, the biblical author rejects the heroic legend as the model for religious leadership. The rite of passage of the ordained requires a breakdown of the human ego so that the one being called is open to the new experiences of the sacred beyond the boundaries of human self-will and power. Moses models the rite of passage of ordination from failed hero to religious leader. His failure as a political hero leads to his transformation into a religious leader in his encounter with God in the burning bush. The process of transformation continues until Moses's face is permanently invaded by the sacred during the revelation at the divine mountain.

We have also seen that the Mosaic office influenced the literary composition of the Torah, because the story of Moses is fashioned to clarify two contrasting offices of ordination, one prophetic and charismatic in nature and the other priestly and ritualistic. The twofold focus of the biblical authors is evident in the call experience of Moses in Exodus 3–7. The two commissions of Moses explore the distinctive experiences of holiness as a dynamic force and as a ritual resource. The prophetic call of Moses in Exodus 3–4 is grounded in a sudden and unexpected encounter, in which Yahweh invades Moses by appearing to him in the burning bush. The wilderness provides the setting for an introspective commission, which probes personal doubts of adequacy. The process is meant to overcome the power of the human ego in order to authenticate Moses as a charismatic leader. The elders of Israel must recognize the power of God in Moses and acquire faith in him by seeing his charismatic gifts for leadership. The setting of Egypt, rather than the wilderness, sets the stage for the priestly call of Moses in Exodus 6–7. The priestly call lacks the introspection of the prophetic call. The authenticity of the priestly call to ordination is established through a critical study of tradition and genealogy, while the commission of Moses is to be a ritual specialist who mediates divine wonders into the land of Egypt. The result of Moses's priestly call to ordination will be the public displays of judgment on the Egyptians, which will force the Egyptians and Pharaoh to acknowledge Yahweh.

Biblical interpreters in the modern era have concluded that the author of the priestly call of Moses in Exodus 6–7 is not the same person who composed the prophetic call of Moses in Exodus 3–4. Thus, the portrait of Moses in Torah is a composite story from authors with distinct views of ordination and religious leadership, one prophetic and focused on the charismatic word and the other priestly with an emphasis on the performance of rituals to mediate holiness into the profane world. The two authors likely represent competing traditions of worship and religious leadership in ancient Israel. The portrait of Moses in Exodus 3–7, however, does not allow the reader to pick and choose between the competing traditions, since both call experiences are now woven into the one story of Moses's ordination. The result is that the present form of Torah includes distinct experiences of holiness combined into the one office of ordination. The process of call to the Mosaic office includes both the charismatic experience of holiness as the numinous, which prompts critical self-reflection with regard to motive and ego, and the ritual appropriation of holiness through the critical study of tradition and liturgy. The distinctive experiences of holiness within the call process lay the foundation for the ordination to the charismatic word and to the ritual mediation of the sacrament in Christian tradition.

The competing experiences of the call to ordination are common in students at my seminary. The process of the call to ordination often follows the story of Moses. Many enter seminary in the wake of a charismatic encounter with holiness as the numinous. The decision to enter seminary is usually part of a process of critical self-reflection that is very similar to the prophetic call of Moses in Exodus 3–4. Once in seminary, however, the call experience is shaped by a critical study of tradition, both through the seminary curriculum and in judicatory boards of ordination. Throughout the educational process, the focus is more on the power of holiness as a ritual resource, in which candidates are expected to become ritual practitioners of holiness through liturgy, sacrament, and administration. Often, my students state that the authentic experience of holiness was the initial charismatic encounter of the numinous and that the ritual power of holiness acquired through professional training is of secondary value—sometimes even viewed as a hurdle to be overcome so that they can enter the ministry. The model of ordination that arises from the Mosaic office indicates that nothing could be further from the truth. The call experience of Moses underscores that the distinct experiences of holiness work in tandem to prepare him for ordination.

The following chapters will explore in more detail the ways in which the twofold character of the Mosaic office, as prophet and as priest, provide the biblical model for ordination to the word and sacrament in Christian tradition. Chapter 4 will interpret the role of Moses as a charismatic teacher of the divine word in the book of Deuteronomy, where he is invaded by holiness as a dynamic force. The chapter will also trace the influence of the charismatic interpretation of the Mosaic office in the New Testament. Chapter 5 will describe the function of Moses as a priestly mediator in the book of Leviticus, where holiness is a ritual resource. The chapter will also include a description of the continuing influence of the priestly view of the Mosaic office in the New Testament. The interpretation of the Mosaic office will clarify that the two portrayals of Moses in Torah as prophet and as priest cannot be harmonized with each other. Instead, they are held in tension in the person of Moses, who represents the one office of ordination to the prophetic word and to the priestly sacramental rituals. This creative tension provides the model for a biblical theology of ordination to the word and sacrament in Christian tradition.

RESOURCES FOR FURTHER STUDY

Brueggemann, W. *The Book of Exodus*. NIB I. Nashville, Tenn.: Abingdon, 1994.

Childs, B. S. *The Book of Exodus: A Critical, Theological Commentary*. OTL. Philadelphia: Westminster, 1974.

Coats, G. W. *Moses: Heroic Man, Man of God*. JSOTSup 57. Sheffield, England: Sheffield Academic Press, 1988.

Dozeman, T. *Exodus*. The Eerdmans Criticial Commentary. Edited by D. N. Freedman. Grand Rapids: Wm B. Eerdmans Pub., 2008.

Durham, J. I. *Exodus*. WBC 3. Waco, Tex.: Word Books, 1987.

Fretheim, T. E. *Exodus: Interpretation*. Louisville, Ky.: John Knox, 1991.

Gowan, D. E. *Theology in Exodus: Biblical Theology in the Form of a Commentary*. Louisville, Ky.: Westminster/John Knox, 1994.

Greenberg, M. *Understanding Exodus*. New York: Behrman House, 1969.

Houtman, C. *Exodus*. Volume 1: *Historical Commentary of the Old Testament*. Kampen, Netherlands: Kok, 1993.

————. *Exodus*. Volume 2: *Historical Commentary of the Old Testament*. Kampen, Netherlands: Kok, 1995.

————. *Exodus*. Volume 3: *Historical Commentary of the Old Testament*. Kampen, Netherlands: Kok, 2000.

Meyers, C. *Exodus*. NCBC. Cambridge: Cambridge University Press, 2005.

Noth, M. *Exodus: A Commentary*. OTL. Translated by J. S. Bowden. Philadelphia: Westminster, 1962.

Propp, W. H. *Exodus 1–18*. AB 2A. Garden City, N.Y.: Doubleday, 1999.

Sarna, N. *Exodus: The JPS Torah Commentary*. Philadelphia: Jewish Publication Society, 1991.

Van Seters, J. *The Life of Moses: The Yahwist as Historian in Exodus–Numbers*. Louisville, Ky.: Westminster/John Knox, 1994.

Holiness and the Ordination to the Divine Word in Deuteronomy and in the New Testament

Moses functions as a charismatic teacher of the divine word in the book of Deuteronomy. Our aim in this chapter is to describe the theology of holiness in the book of Deuteronomy in order to interpret the understanding of ordination that is modeled by Moses as he teaches the Israelites. We will also trace the same theology of holiness in selected New Testament literature. The religious experience of the numinous in the work of Rudolf Otto will guide the interpretation. The interpretation of Moses as a charismatic teacher of the divine word will require a broad study of the relationship of the sacred and the profane in the book of Deuteronomy. For this reason, the chapter will be separated into the following sections: The introduction will summarize the literary context of the book of Deuteronomy. "The Separate Quality of Holiness" will explore the transcendence of God. "The Sacred and the Profane" will examine the way in which holiness invades the profane world of humans through the divine voice. The broader study of holiness and the divine voice will allow for an interpretation of "The Sacred and Ordination."

The Literary Setting of the Book of Deuteronomy

The literary context is important for interpreting the teaching on holiness in the book of Deuteronomy and for understanding its implications for the ordination to the word in Christian tradition. Deuteronomy is the last of the five books of Torah: Genesis, Exodus, Leviticus, Numbers, and Deuteronomy. The book of Genesis provides the prehistory of the Israelite nation. It begins with the creation of the world and the formation of the nations (Gn 1–11) before it narrows in focus to trace the story of the ancestors Abraham, Isaac, and Jacob (Gn 12–50). The books of Exodus, Leviticus, and Numbers have a national focus, as compared to the family stories in Genesis. They recount the original experience of salvation from Egypt, including the exodus from Egypt (Ex 1–15), the revelation of God at the divine mountain (Ex 16–40; Leviticus; Nm 1–10), and the wilderness journey toward the promised land of Canaan (Nm 11–36). These books recount the story of the first generation of Israelites, who experience directly the salvation of God but reject it by fearing to follow God into the promised land of Canaan (Nm 13–14).

The book of Deuteronomy is set apart in time from the story in Exodus, Leviticus, and Numbers. The original events of salvation are now history, and the participants in those events are no longer present, except for Moses.[1] The literature consists of teachings by Moses on the last day of his life to the second generation of Israelites. In this role, Moses embodies the charismatic aspect of the Mosaic office, which was central to his prophetic call in Exodus 3–4. Moses recounts the experiences of the exodus, the wilderness journey, and, most important, the appearance of God on Mount Horeb, when the law was first revealed to the Israelites. His aim is to recount the past events of salvation history in order to persuade the present generation of Israelites to follow Yahweh, even though they have no firsthand experience of the primary events.

The book of Deuteronomy explores the problem of salvation in a historical context, when the people of God are removed from the original event of salvation and the primary experience of revelation. How does the second generation of Israelites embrace the power and holiness of God demonstrated in the exodus and revealed at Mount Horeb, when they have not experienced these events themselves? The theology of holiness and the idealization of Moses as a teacher in the book of Deuteronomy offer a solution to the problem of history and religious experience. The ordination of Moses to the divine word will play a vital role in relating a past event of salvation to the religious experience of later generations.

We will see that the same problem of history and religious experience also emerges in the New Testament and continues in Christian tradition. How is the saving experience of the historical Jesus passed on to later generations, who have not experienced the events of Jesus' life and passion? The problem of history and religious experience is already evident in the statement of Thomas immediately after the passion of Jesus, when he declares at the close of the Gospel of John: "Unless I see the mark of the nails in his hands, and put my finger in the mark of the nails, and my hand in his side, I will not believe" (Jn 20:25). Rudolf Otto poses the problem of Thomas for all Christians: "How can we, too, come to experience in Him [Jesus] 'holiness made manifest[?]' "[2] Otto concludes that the reception of the holiness of Jesus by humans who are now removed in time from his life will require the invasion of the numinous spirit, made manifest by prophets. Otto's conclusion for Christians is already anticipated in the book of Deuteronomy.

The Separate Quality of Holiness

God is transcendent in the book of Deuteronomy, dwelling in heaven and not on earth. The transcendence of God accentuates the nature of holiness as separate from the profane world. The cultic liturgy for the tithe in Deuteronomy 26:12–15 provides the central teaching on the transcendence of God. At the conclusion of the liturgy, the worshiper invokes God with the words:

> Look down from your holy habitation from heaven,
> and bless your people Israel
> and the ground that you have given us.

The liturgy allows for several conclusions about God and holiness in the book of Deuteronomy. The most significant insight is the proclamation that God dwells in heaven and not on earth, requiring that the deity look down upon the earth. Heaven and earth are distinct realms. The request of the worshiper for a blessing on Israel and on the ground accentuates the separation between heaven and earth. Blessing must emanate from heaven; it cannot emerge from the profane world itself. Heaven, moreover, is also the location of holiness. It is God's "holy habitation," making explicit the distinction between the sacred realm of heaven and the profane earth.

The transcendent view in Deuteronomy of God, dwelling in heaven, continues into the New Testament literature. The synoptic Gospels assume the separation of God from creation by locating the deity in heaven. Matthew repeatedly refers to God as the "Father in heaven" (e.g., Mt 6:1, 26; 7:21; 12:50; ; 16:17; 18:14). The phrase also occurs infrequently in Mark (11:25) and in Luke (10:21). The Gospels' writers further agree that the declaration of God during the baptism of Jesus was a "voice from heaven" (Mk 1:11; Lk 3:22; Mt 3:17). Even Jesus must lift his eyes to heaven in order to pray to God (Lk 9:16). The identity of God as the Father in heaven serves the same function as the references to heaven in the book of Deuteronomy: separating the deity from humans on the earth. The confrontation between Jesus and his opponents over the baptism of John illustrates further the separate quality of the region of heaven from the profane world of humans. Jesus equates heaven with divine authority in contrast to human authority in the profane world: "John's baptism—was it from heaven or from men?" (Mk 11:30–33).

The Lord's Prayer in Matthew 6:9–10 (see also Lk 11:2) even provides points of contact with the prayer of the tithe in Deuteronomy 26:12–15:

> Our Father, who is in heaven,
> let your name be made holy, your kingdom come, and your
>   will be done
> as in heaven, so on earth.

The imagery of God as the Father in heaven is prominent in the prayer. The closing line specifies that heaven is separate from the earth. And the middle line of the prayer indicates that holiness is a characteristic of heaven. The prayer states that the presence of God, or at least the divine name, is separate from the profane world of the earth.

The division between heaven and earth provides the background for interpreting the separation between God and humans. Humans are not part of the world of heaven. They are creatures of the earth. Deuteronomy 4:32 states: "God created human beings on the earth." Thus, they dwell under heaven and not in it. This is true for all the nations and for the Israelites (Dt 2:25, 4:19). The apostle Paul echoes the same teaching: "But who indeed are you, a human being, to argue with God? Will what is molded say to the one who molds it, 'Why have you made me like this?' " (Rom 9:20).

Humans may try to participate in the sacred realm of heaven by creating strong cities that are "fortified to the heavens" (Dt 9:1) or by worshiping the "host of heaven" (Dt 4:19, 17:3). But in the book of Deuteronomy, such actions are an abomination which only create further separation between God and humans, prompting divine anger that leads to destruction. Moses warns the Israelites: "Let nothing that is doomed stick to your hand, in order that Yahweh may turn from his blazing anger" (Dt 13:17). The apostle Paul repeats a similar warning: "For the wrath of God is revealed from heaven against all ungodliness and wickedness of those who by their wickedness suppress the truth" (Rom 1:18).

The overview of heaven and earth and of God and humans indicates two kinds of separation in the book of Deuteronomy. The first is the sacred and the profane. These realms are clearly distinct, with God dwelling in heaven and humans on earth. The quest for humans to locate God in the profane world through political power or in worshiping aspects of creation establishes further distance between God and humans. The second separation explores the contrast between the pure and the impure. The divide between the pure and the impure is stated through the imagery of the alienation of God from humans, expressed with the personal language of passion and emotion, which recalls the charismatic character of the numinous in the work of Rudolf Otto. God is the source of raw emotion in the book of Deuteronomy, becoming jealous when humans make gods of themselves or of some aspect of the profane world (Dt 6:15). The jealousy of God produces divine anger on earth. Moses warns the Israelites that Yahweh is an impassioned God (Dt 6:15). Moses, himself, is in dread of this fierce anger (Dt 9:19). And he cautions the people that the worship of the profane world will bring forth "the anger of Yahweh." It will "shut up the heavens, so that there will be no rain and the land will yield no fruit; then you will perish quickly off the good land that Yahweh is giving you" (Dt 11:17). The teaching of Moses resurfaces in the book of Hebrews, when the author repeats images from Deuteronomy 4:24, describing God as a consuming fire (Heb 12:29) and warning his audience that "it is a fearful thing to fall into the hand of the living God" (Heb 10:31).

The ideal human in the book of Deuteronomy is someone who knows his or her place in the created order. The worshiper in the liturgy of the tithe and in the Lord's Prayer understands the difference between heaven and earth and between God and humans. God is addressed in heaven. Heaven is the source of holiness. The worshiper is firmly situated in the profane world. The worshiper knows that heaven, not earth, is the source of life (Dt 11:17, 28:12; Mt 6:9–11).

The Sacred and the Profane

The separation of the sacred and the profane is not the final word in the book of Deuteronomy any more than it is in the New Testament. Deuteronomy 10:14 states that heaven and earth belong to God. The challenge is to describe how holiness invades the profane world of humans through time and in human history. The focus on history in the book of Deuteronomy presents Moses with two goals in his teaching. The first is to recount how the holiness of God claimed the first generation of Israelites in the past events of the exodus, the revelation at Mount Horeb, and the wilderness journey. The second goal is to explain what the past events of salvation mean for the present generation of Israelites, who have not experienced them.

The two goals of the book of Deuteronomy address the problem of history and religious experience, which continues in Christian tradition, where the mission of Jesus is also a past event for contemporary Christians. We have already noted that Rudolf Otto summarizes the problem of history and religious experience with the question: "How can we[,] too, come to experience . . . 'holiness made manifest'?" We will see that the book of Deuteronomy provides the paradigm for how the people of God experience holiness throughout history and that the ordination to the divine word is crucial to the process.

The Dynamic Power of Divine Election

The gulf between the sacred and the profane is overcome in the book of Deuteronomy by divine election. The Hebrew word for election, *baḥar*, describes the act of choosing. Election is a personal choice, unrestrained by any structures or expectations. The word is used almost exclusively in the book of Deuteronomy to describe God's choice to invade the profane world and to claim the Israelite people. It is used in Deuteronomy 23:15–16, however, in a law concerning runaway slaves, which provides a starting point for our interpretation.

Deuteronomy 23:15–16 illustrates the dynamic and the unrestrained power implied in the word *election*. The law states that runaway slaves may not be returned to their masters. The law continues by describing where escaped slaves may live: "in any place they choose [*baḥar*] in any one of your towns, where they please; you shall not oppress them." The choice of residency for a slave is personal ("in any place they choose"), it is unrestrained ("in any one of your towns"), and, in the end, it is unpredictable ("where they please"). The slave has absolute freedom in electing a place of residency. The choice of residency cannot be controlled by any of the Israelites ("you shall not oppress them"). The same personal, dynamic, unrestrained, and unpredictable power also characterizes God's election of the Israelite people. The dynamic character of divine election in the book of Deuteronomy is rooted in a charismatic interpretation of holiness, which overlaps in many ways with Otto's description of the numinous.

The book of Deuteronomy describes two acts of divine election, one in the past and another in the present. The past election of God is the salvation of the first generation of Israelites through the events of the exodus, the revelation at Mount Horeb, and the wilderness journey. These events occurred once in history, and they cannot be repeated in the experience of the later generation of Israelites. The second election of God is the selection of a sanctuary, where God chooses to place the divine name. The election of a sanctuary repeats throughout history as the Israelites continue to engage the dynamic power of holiness in worship. The interaction of the two forms of election allows the second generation of Israelites to embrace the past salvation of God, even though they have not experienced the events themselves. The ordination of Moses as a teacher of the divine word is crucial for relating the two forms of divine election in the religious experience of the people. His charismatic and persuasive speech recreates the original experience of salvation for the later generation of Israelites. The problem of unrepeatable history and ongoing religious experience is also central to the New Testament as the early charismatic teachers, like Paul, seek to proclaim the continuing power of Jesus long after his historical ministry.

The Past Election of Israel in the Exodus and in the Revelation at Mount Horeb

The book of Deuteronomy describes the election of the ancestors as an unrepeatable historical event, in which God rescued them from Egyptian slavery and infused the people with holiness at Mount Horeb. The historical election of the ancestors is a free and unpredictable divine choice. Deuteronomy 7:7 states that the election of the ancestors was not because they were more numerous than other people. In fact, they were the fewest of all people. The arbitrary nature of God's election is an unpredictable act of love. Deuteronomy 10:15 states: Even though heaven and earth belong to Yahweh, God "set his heart in love on your ancestors alone and chose you." There is no logical or moral reason for the divine election of the ancestors. It is, rather, the result of the free and personal choice of God. The dynamic character of divine election reinforces the work of Rudolf Otto, where the invasion of the numinous into the profane world is also a gift which defies predictable moral boundaries or any other form of human reasoning. Paul echoes the same insight when he reminds the Corinthians that they do not represent the wise, powerful, or noble of birth in the Roman world, which leads to his conclusion that God's election is unpredictable and even foolish, since it targets the weak, the lowly, and the despised of the world (1 Cor 1:18–31).

The invasion of the sacred into the profane world in the revelation at Mount Horeb further strengthens the parallels to Otto's description of the numinous. The Israelites' experience of God at Mount Horeb is thoroughly charismatic. The voice of God is a gift that can only be received. God states to Moses: "I will let [the people] hear my words" (Dt 4:10). The voice of God is unmediated and personal, pressing itself upon the people. Moses describes the experience as a direct encounter with the deity: "Yahweh spoke with you face to face at the mountain, out of the fire" (Dt 5:4). The experience embraces the entire nation equally; it is not restricted to a select group nor controlled through rituals. The whole assembly "heard the sound of words" (Dt 5:22, 4:12). These are also characteristics of the numinous, which is able to press itself upon a person as a direct and personal spiritual gift.

The transformation of the people of Israel at Mount Horeb continues the comparison to the experience of the numinous. Holiness directly invades all of the Israelites at Mount Horeb, making the nation a holy people and God's private possession as a result of their election. Moses declares to the Israelites: "For you are a holy people to Yahweh your God; it is you Yahweh has chosen out of all the people on earth to be his people, his treasured possession" (Dt 14:2; see also 7:6, 14:21, 26:18). The holy status of the people at Mount Horeb is evident in their transformed character. God predicts that hearing the divine voice will instill fear in the people: "I will let [the people] hear my words, so that they may learn to fear me as long as they live on earth" (Dt 4:10).

The fear of God emerges as the most important characteristic of a holy people in the book of Deuteronomy (e.g., Dt 4:10; 5:5, 29; 6:2, 13, 24; 8:6). It derives from hearing the voice of God, which illuminates the nature of religious experience. In hearing the voice of Yahweh at Mount Horeb, the people learn that God is wholly other and cannot be associated with any object in the profane world. The people realize further that the direct experience of God, as speech, is too dangerous for humans. They declare to Moses: "For who is there of all flesh that has heard the voice of the living God speaking out of fire, as we have, and remained alive?" (Dt 5:26). "If we hear the voice of Yahweh our God any longer, we shall die" (Dt 5:25). God approves of the Israelites' fear, stating to Moses: "If only they had such a mind as this, to fear me and to keep my commandments always" (Dt 5:28). The apostle Paul extends the teaching of the book of Deuteronomy when he states to the Corinthians: "Since we have these promises, beloved, let us cleanse ourselves from every defilement of body and of spirit, making holiness perfect in the fear of God" (2 Cor 7:1).

The Israelites' fear of God is neither a form of morality nor a psychological disposition. It is a primal experience, recalling the state of creature-consciousness in the work of Rudolf Otto, with its sense of dread and awe. Both are intended to describe the essence of religious experience as a unique quality (sui generis), which arises from the direct invasion of the sacred. The difference is that the experience of the divine voice at Mount Horeb is unrepeatable, as compared to the numinous, with its ability to invade humans through time.

The charismatic interpretation of holiness in the book of Deuteronomy influences the New Testament authors in the description of Jesus and his disciples. The mission of Jesus is an unrepeatable invasion of the sacred into the profane, which is often described with the same personal and dynamic language of the numinous: "For God so loved the world that he gave his only son" (Jn 3:16). The baptism of Jesus (Mk 1:9–11) and the story of the transfiguration (Mk 9:2–10) are unrepeatable events of salvation, in which the voice of God from heaven claims Jesus as the "beloved son." The transfiguration story in Luke even uses the language of divine election, recalling the book of Deuteronomy: "This is my son, my chosen" (Lk 9:35). The disciples' encounter with Jesus is often described as a primal experience of the numinous. After Peter's confession in Matthew, "You are the Messiah, the son of the Living God," Jesus responds: "Flesh and blood has not revealed this to you, but my Father in heaven" (Mt 16:17). The reference to the "heavenly Father," according to Otto, is a daring paradox about the character of God: "He who is 'in heaven' is yet 'our Father.'"[3] Otto concludes that such a paradox can only be known through the experience of the numinous. And the experience leads to awe and fear, as in the reaction of the disciples to the transfiguration of Jesus: "They did not know what to do, for they were terrified" (Mk 9:6).

The Present Election of a Sanctuary for the Divine Name

The divine election of the ancestors in the book of Deuteronomy is a charismatic gift, requiring the experience of the voice of God at Mount Horeb. Such a direct encounter with God cannot be repeated for any future generation of Israelites. In the same way, the mission of Jesus and the experience of the disciples at the transfiguration is a past event in Christian tradition. It, too, cannot be repeated. Yet, neither the book of Deuteronomy nor the New Testament is content to dwell on the past invasion of holiness into the profane world. Both bodies of literature insist that the numinous experience of holiness must continue for later generations. The book of Deuteronomy forges the solution to the problem of history and ongoing religious experience through the theology of the divine name in the sanctuary, which must be experienced by later worshipers. The theology of the divine name also influences New Testament writers, who seek to relate the life and passion of Jesus to later Christian worshipers by proclaiming the name of Jesus. The dynamic relationship between a past event of salvation and contemporary religious experience is crucial to the office of the ordination to the word in Christian tradition.

God provides the setting in the book of Deuteronomy for relating the original experience of salvation to the later generation of Israelites with an additional form of election. God chooses to place the divine name in a sanctuary, which will allow the Israelites to participate in the past events of the exodus and the revelation at Mount Horeb through worship. God states to the Israelites: "You shall seek the place that Yahweh your God will choose [bahar] out of all your tribes as his habitation to put his Name [shem] there" (Dt 12:5). The divine election of a sanctuary for the name of God is prominent in the book of Deuteronomy. It is the central motif in the chapter on worship (Dt 12:5, 11, 14, 18, 21, 26). It is the location for the tithe (Dt 14:24, 25), the yearly festivals (Dt 16:2, 6, 7, 11, 15, 16), the legal proceedings (Dt 17:8, 10), the workplace of the Levites (Dt 18:6), the gift of first fruits (Dt 26:2), and the reading of the law (Dt 31:11).

The name of God does not represent the same intensity of religious experience as the direct encounter with the voice of God at Mount Horeb. The worshiper does not experience God or the divine voice directly by traveling back in time to the original events of the exodus. Yet the name of God in the sanctuary echoes the original encounter. The difference in the direct experience of Yahweh as opposed to the name is illustrated in the liturgy of the tithe, which we examined earlier (Dt 26:12–15). The liturgy of the tithe takes place in the sanctuary "before Yahweh." Yet the direct voice of God is removed from the worshiper, since Yahweh now resides in heaven. The divine name in the sanctuary represents a modified quality of the divine presence of the God of the exodus within the sanctuary, which allows for continuity with the past revelation of God at Mount Horeb, without repeating the event. The Lord's Prayer repeats the structure of the liturgy of the tithe by also invoking the divine name, rather than the deity directly: "Let your Name be made holy."

The name of God in the sanctuary represents the charismatic power of retelling the original story of salvation. Moses forges the connections among the original voice of God, the retelling of the story of salvation, and its eventual recording as scripture for later generations in his description of the experience at Mount Horeb: "You heard the sound of words but saw no form; there was only a voice. He [God] declared to you his covenant, which he charged you to observe, that is the ten commandments, and he wrote them on two stone tablets" (Dt 4:13). The name of God in the sanctuary is the proclamation of salvation, which becomes preserved in a written record of the original events. The tablets of stone are not the same as the experience at Mount Horeb, yet their content provides continuity with the original experience. Thus, Moses encourages the Israelites to follow the law (e.g., Dt 6:2, 24; 8:6; 13:5), and, in so doing, they also observe the name of God (e.g., Dt 6:13, 10:20). The same dynamic relationship between the historical Jesus and his continuing power is evident throughout the book of Acts, when the disciples proclaim the name of Jesus as a source of salvation after his historical ministry (Acts 2:38, 3:6, 4:10, 5:40, 8:12, 9:27, 16:18).

The relationship between proclamation and the original experience of salvation is even more dynamic. Repeatedly, Moses teaches the second generation that the divine voice at Mount Horeb, now codified as scripture, is the lifeline between the original event of salvation and their experience of it. He teaches the people that the observance of written law can even instill the fear of God in them, thus transmitting the very essence of religious experience from one generation to the next (e.g., Dt 6:2, 13, 24; 8:6). The transmission of the fear of the divine takes place in the sanctuary of the name, as one generation teaches the next about the past acts of salvation history recorded in scripture. Moses encourages the Israelites to teach their children the meaning of salvation by recounting the exodus and the revelation of law at Mount Horeb (Dt 6:20–25). The same dynamic relationship between scripture and a past event of salvation continues into the New Testament, where it is illustrated most clearly in the conclusion to the Gospel of John: "These things have been written in order that you may believe that Jesus is the Messiah, the Son of God and that through your faith in him you may have life" (Jn 20:31). As in the book of Deuteronomy, the Gospel of John is the lifeline between the historical Jesus and the later experience of him. The numinous experience of Jesus through scripture is not the same as that of the first generation of disciples, for whom Jesus performed many more signs (Jn 20:30), yet it is able to produce life.

The result of proclaiming the past events of salvation, teaching scripture, and instilling the fear of God in children is that every generation may be infused with the same holiness of God as the first generation, who experienced the divine voice at Mount Horeb. Thus, election is not confined to the ancestors who undertook the exodus and who experienced the divine voice at Mount Horeb. It reaches through time to the next generation: "And because he [God] loved your ancestors, he chose [bahar] their descendants after them" (Dt 4:37). Moses explains further that the intergenerational character of election makes the descendants of the exodus generation a holy people like their ancestors: "Today Yahweh has obtained your agreement: to be his treasured people as he promised you; . . . and for you to be a people holy to Yahweh your God, as he promised." Philippians 2:10 extends the same dynamic view of the holiness of the divine name into the New Testament in this hymn line: "so that at the name of Jesus every knee should bend, in heaven and on earth and under the earth."

The charismatic transmission of holiness from one generation to the next also informs the New Testament authors. Holiness in the form of the Holy Spirit infuses the disciples of Jesus at Pentecost (Acts 2). Yet, the author of 1 Peter also describes post-Easter Christians, those who have not encountered the historical Jesus, as "chosen" by God and as "holy" (1 Pt 2:9). The "holy ones" (saints) even becomes the designation for

Christians, especially in the writings of the apostle Paul (e.g., 1 Cor 16:15; Phil 4:23), recalling the language of Moses to the second generation of Israelites in the book of Deuteronomy. The title "saints," according to Rudolf Otto, arises from the ongoing experience of the numinous by early Christians, illustrated most dramatically in the apostle Paul's own encounter on the road to Damascus, where he, like the Israelites at Mount Horeb, hears a voice from heaven without seeing any form (Acts 9:1–19). The experience illustrates that saints are those who have participated in the mystery, which creates an "unambiguous antithesis to the profane," according to Otto. The apostle Paul attributes the charismatic infusion of holiness in Christians to a predestined election. But, as in the book of Deuteronomy, divine election is neither rational nor controllable. It is, rather, a numinous encounter, arising from the experience of having been chosen. Otto explains: "It is an immediate and pure expression of the actual religious experience of grace. Not an achievement, but a gift received."[4]

The interpretation of holiness in the book of Deuteronomy resists clear ritual structure or even confinement to a specific sanctuary. Thus, the sanctuary of the name is impossible to locate in any particular town or temple within the book of Deuteronomy. Interpreters debate whether the sanctuary is in Shechem, Gilgal, Mount Ebal, or Jerusalem. Yet, the image and the architecture of the sanctuary of the name do emerge from the literature. It is a stark structure. All visual images are forbidden in the sanctuary. Moses cautions the Israelites against making any idol in the form of any figure, whether human, animal, or bird (Dt 4:15–20). The prohibition against images reinforces the absence of holiness in any of the objects within the sanctuary. Holiness resides dynamically in the people of God; it is not a ritual resource within any sacramental objects. Even the tablets of stone are not accorded a sacred status. Deuteronomy 10:1–5 states that the tablets of stone are placed in the ark. But neither the tablets nor the ark are clearly placed within the sanctuary, nor are they described as holy.

Deuteronomy 31:14–15 provides a glimpse into what the sanctuary of the name would look like. It is an impermanent structure, described as the tent of meeting. The tent is devoid of furniture or any cultic objects. It is an empty space, recalling the religious experience of the numinous as a void in the writing of Rudolf Otto. God is not even described as entering the tent. Instead, the divine cloud would descend at the entrance of the tent in order for Moses to hear the divine voice. The tent of meeting is the location where the Israelites cultivate the holiness that is within them by strengthening their fear of God through the reading of scripture and the observance of law (Dt 31:11). The sanctuary, conceived as the place of the name, underscores that worship is a continuing, albeit modified, experience of the voice of God at Mount Horeb, now transmitted through the reading of scripture and the persuasive teaching of a charismatic leader. With such a dynamic view of worship and holiness, the exact location of the place of the name becomes less important. It is, rather, the experience of teaching and community relationships that take center stage, much like the teaching of Jesus in the Gospel of Matthew: "For where two or three are gathered in my Name, I am there with them" (Mt 18:20).

The Sacred and Ordination

The Mosaic office in the book of Deuteronomy is charismatic and prophetic in nature. Moses is a persuasive teacher, who is able to forge connections between a past event of salvation and the present religious experience of a later generation of Israelites. The charismatic ordination of Moses in Deuteronomy is rooted in his confrontation with the numinous fire of God from the burning bush in Exodus 3–4, where he underwent a prophetic call experience. In this section, we will explore how Moses models the ordination to the divine word in the book of Deuteronomy and lays the foundation for the ordination to the word in Christian tradition.

The Origin of the Ordination to the Divine Word

The prophetic call of Moses in Exodus 3–4 emphasized the need for the people of Israel to acquire faith in Moses, which meant that they would recognize his divine commission through his persuasive speech. The central role of the faith of the Israelites in Moses continues in the book of Deuteronomy. The authority of Moses and, indeed, his ordination arise from the choice of the people in the book of Deuteronomy and not from God. Deuteronomy 5:22–33 recounts the process by which Moses acquires authority and an office of leadership at Mount Horeb. The passage begins with the statement that all of the Israelites heard the voice of God at Mount Horeb: "Yahweh spoke with a loud voice to your whole assembly at the mountain, out of the fire, the cloud, and the thick darkness" (Dt 5:22). The people acknowledge to Moses their successful encounter with God: "Look, Yahweh our God has shown us his glory and greatness, and we have heard his voice out of the fire. Today we have seen that God may speak to someone and the person may live." The statement emphasizes that all of the Israelites hear the voice of God, become a holy people, and acquire the fear of God from the religious experience of encountering the divine voice. They confirm their newly acquired fear by stating to Moses: "This great fire will consume us; if we hear the voice of Yahweh our God any longer" (Dt 5:25). It is out of their fear of God that they select Moses to represent them in receiving any further words from God: "Go near, you yourself, and hear all that Yahweh our God will say. Then tell us everything that Yahweh our God tells you, and we will listen and do it." God approves of the actions of the Israelites in choosing Moses to represent them: "I have heard the words of this people, which they have spoken to you; they are right in all that they have spoken. If only they had such a mind as this, to fear me and to keep all my commandments always" (Dt 5:28–29).

Thus, Deuteronomy 5:22–33 describes the origin of the ordination to the divine word in the book of Deuteronomy. God does not select Moses. Rather, the people of God choose Moses for a position of leadership. They select Moses because they fear God. The divine fear in the people is the result of their encounter with God, in which holiness in the form of the divine voice invaded the Israelite nation as a whole. Moses shares in the same holiness as the people, because he, too, has heard the divine voice at Mount Horeb. As a result, the ordination of Moses to the divine word is not a separation between a sacred clergy and a profane laity, since the people of God are already holy. The special office of Moses is, rather, a separate function that he assumes in transmitting the word of God to the people.

The functional nature of Moses's leadership does not change his character. Rather, it defines his responsibility in relationship to the whole people of God, who are already holy like Moses. Rudolf Otto clarifies the distinction between Moses and the Israelites, which results from Moses's ordination, with an analogy to art. Most humans, he notes, have the receptive ability to respond to and to judge art. But few humans are able to create art. If we think of the encounter with holiness at Mount Horeb as an aesthetic experience, the result is that all of the Israelite people become art critics, since they acquire the capacity to judge the authenticity of similar experiences. The functional ordination of Moses to transmit additional divine words to the Israelite people requires that he become an artist in addition to being an art critic. Thus, the responsibility of Moses is not simply to receive the gift of holiness through additional divine words. But, like an artist, he must also recreate the divine words for the entire people of God, who, because of their holy status, are already art critics. The holiness of the people of Israel allows them to receive the words from Moses and to evaluate their authenticity even though they are not able to create the speech themselves. For Otto, the responsibility to receive the divine voice and to create it anew for others is a prophetic office that is rooted in the dynamic power of the numinous.[5]

The Responsibilities of the Ordination to the Divine Word

The ordination of Moses in the book of Deuteronomy models the responsibilities associated with the ordination to the word in Christian tradition. Moses's primary responsibility in the book of Deuteronomy is to teach scripture to the people. But Moses also takes on the role of intercessor for the people. Both roles of teacher and of intercessor are rooted in charismatic gifts of persuasion. Other responsibilities of the ordination to the divine word are associated with the roles of the elders and of the Levitical priests in the book of Deuteronomy.

MOSES THE CHARISMATIC TEACHER. Moses is a persuasive teacher in the book of Deuteronomy. Many interpreters structure the book of Deuteronomy as sermons by Moses (Dt 1:1–4:43, 4:44–28:68, 28:69–30:20) in which he recounts the past experience of salvation and teaches the divine law to a later generation of Israelites. Moses himself articulates his vocation as one of teaching scripture, and, in the process, he also equates the people's selection of him as divine will: "Yahweh charged me at that time [at Horeb] to teach you statutes and ordinances for you to observe" (Dt 4:14). It is not enough for Moses to simply teach, however, his office is also more charismatic, requiring that he persuade the Israelites of the continuing power of the exodus and the effectiveness of scripture as a resource for authentic religious experience. Thus, the rhetoric of Moses's teaching is forceful, demanding attention ("Hear, O Israel"). It includes pleadings ("give heed"), warnings ("do not forget"), and inspiration ("you will be the most blessed of peoples"). Such persuasive teaching is tied to the dynamic power of holiness as the numinous. It empowers the Israelites to recognize holiness in the teaching of Moses.

The rhetoric of persuasion within the ordination to the divine word gives rise to a dynamic interaction between the speaker and the people of God, because all of the Israelites are already holy. The fear of God resides in all of the people (e.g., Dt 7:6; 14:2, 21). The aim of Moses in the book of Deuteronomy, therefore, is not to transmit holiness to the people in the form of a sacramental ritual. It is, rather, to bring the people to the full consciousness of the holiness that already resides within them as a result of their election. The teaching of scripture and its charismatic proclamation are the means for achieving the goal. Thus, wisdom and understanding become central motifs in the book of Deuteronomy, since they indicate the coming to consciousness of the holy people of God. Moses encourages the people: "You must observe [the statutes and the ordinances] diligently, for this will show your wisdom and discernment" (Dt 4:6). Rudolf Otto states that the recognition of the pure feeling of holiness is the task of theology. Those who are called to the task require the visionary intuition of a prophet, which is receptive to "the pressure of the numinous experience and nothing else."[6] Otto adds further that, in the ministry of Jesus and in the early church, the prophetic intuition of the numinous is a gift of the spirit.

The function of the leader ordained to the divine word is not simply to bring the people to the full consciousness of their election; it is also to protect the holiness of God in the people, since it brings health to the people. Holiness resides in the relationship between the Israelites and God, which was established at Mount Horeb. The Israelites became a personal possession of God's in that event, which brings them into a covenantal relationship with God (e.g., Dt 4:13, 23, 31; 5:2, 3). The holiness of the Israelites is protected when the people carefully maintain their covenantal relationship with God and with each other, and thus they become ethical agents for God in the world. It is not enough that Moses teach the law. It is equally important that the people actively hear the teaching and allow the words to penetrate into their hearts. They must love God with their whole hearts and their neighbors as themselves (e.g., Dt 6:5, 11:1). Thus, worship in the sanctuary of the name, which is focused on the word of God, is heard only when it leads to ethical acts of justice within the community and in the larger world.

Persuasive teaching, therefore, must activate the memory of God in the people. Memory addresses the problem of history and religious experience, since its power derives from the holiness that resides within the people of Israel. It is the dynamic character of memory that allows the Israelites to participate in the past experience of God's saving events in the exodus and in the revelation at Mount Horeb. In this way, memory creates identity. The leader who is ordained to the divine word activates the memory of the people through the teaching of scripture. Moses repeatedly encourages the Israelites: "Remember the days of old, consider the years long past; ask your father and he will inform you; your elders, and they will tell you" (Dt 32:7; see also, e.g., 5:15, 7:18, 8:2, 16:3). The Israelites must remember their slave status in Egypt and God's liberation through the exodus (Dt 5:15), the wilderness journey (Dt 8:2), the sin of the golden calf (Dt 9:7), the cultic festivals (Dt 16:3, 12), and, most important, Yahweh and the covenantal law (Dt 8:18). The memory of God's past events of salvation, moreover, must also be passed on through intergenerational teaching of the law (e.g., Dt 4:9). The same dynamic role of memory continues into the New Testament. The disciples remember events from the life of Jesus (Jn 2:17, 22; 12:16). The apostle Peter remembers the words of Jesus about the baptism of the Holy Spirit, when he experiences the descent of the Spirit on the Gentile (Acts 11:16). The author of Jude encourages Christians to remember the words of the apostles in order to protect their holiness (Jude 1:17–23).

MOSES THE INTERCESSOR. Intercessory prayer also emerges as an important function of Moses in the book of Deuteronomy. We have already seen the important role of persuasive teaching in the portrayal of Moses. Moses employs the same rhetoric of persuasion when his role changes from the teacher, who represents the voice of God to the people, to the intercessor, who represents the concerns of the people to God. The model for intercessory prayer is fashioned in the event of the golden calf at Mount Horeb. The calf is an abomination to Yahweh, prompting the divine anger and the threat of destruction (Dt 9:8–24). Moses risks the danger of approaching God, and he intercedes with Yahweh for the sake of the people: "I lay prostrate before Yahweh when Yahweh intended to destroy you, I prayed to Yahweh" (Dt 9:25–26).

The intercessory prayer of Moses includes many of the same rhetorical features that characterize his teaching of the law to the Israelites. Moses pleads with God: "Do not destroy the people" (Dt 9:26). He even warns God of the unintended consequences of the divine anger: "The land from which you have brought us might say, 'Because Yahweh was not able to bring them into the land that he promised them, and because he hated them, he has brought them out to let them die in the wilderness'" (Dt 9:28). The aim of Moses's intercessory prayer is to prompt the divine memory of past promises to the ancestors, as a means for pacifying the divine anger and changing the outcome of events: "Remember your servants, Abraham, Isaac, and Jacob; pay no attention to the stubbornness of this people" (Dt 9:27).

The theology of the divine name and the power of intercessory prayer also continue in the New Testament. Intercessory prayer in Christian tradition is punctuated with the theology of the name of Jesus: "In the name of Jesus Christ, we pray. Amen." Jesus models the power of prayer in the synoptic Gospels (e.g., Lk 6:12; 9:18, 28), and he encourages his disciples to use intercessory prayer with faith and persuasion (Mk 11:24; Lk 11:9–13). The disciples model intercessory prayer for discernment (Acts 1:24), to receive the spirit (Acts 8:15), and for healing (Acts 9:40, 28:8). The apostle Paul states that the spirit actually takes on the role of persuasion in Christian prayer (Rom 8:26). And the author of James encourages all Christians to use the power of persuasive intercessory prayer (Jas 5:13–18).

The function of intercessory prayer reinforces the charismatic nature of the ordination to the divine word, which emerged in the teaching role of Moses. In teaching the Israelites and in interceding with God, Moses possesses the personal strength of persuasive speech. His authority arises from the power of his character, which has undergone transformation in his prophetic call experience. The aim of Moses's ordination to the divine word is to maintain the relationship between God and the Israelites that was forged in the religious experience of hearing the voice of God at Mount Horeb. The power of Moses to persuade nurtures the memory of God and of the Israelites. God remembers the past promises to the ancestors, while the Israelite people remember the past events of salvation history. The interaction between the memory of God and the memory of the people is possible when the ego of Moses becomes a transparent conductor for the two parties.

ADDITIONAL RESPONSIBILITIES AND OFFICES OF ORDINATION. The more specific tasks of the ordained are not spelled out in the book of Deuteronomy beyond the idealization of Moses. An incomplete sketch of representative activities and responsibilities emerges from the role of the elders and the Levitical priests, information which is scattered throughout the book of Deuteronomy. The Levitical priests and the elders are responsible for interpreting the law (Dt 31:9–13, 26). Thus, most of their duties are associated with adjudicating disputes over the law (Dt 17:8–13), including conflicts over the land (Dt 19:17) and murder (Dt 21:1–9). The Levitical priests must teach the law to the king (Dt 17:14–20) and the people (Dt 24:8–9). They must also evaluate the legitimacy of war (Dt 20:2) and supervise rituals at the sanctuary (Dt 12:15–19, 26:1–15).

Conclusion

The ordination to the divine word in the book of Deuteronomy is anchored in the revelation of God at Mount Horeb. The original invasion of holiness into the profane world is idealized as a direct experience of divine speech at Mount Horeb. The book of Deuteronomy teaches that, in hearing the divine word at Mount Horeb, the exodus generation became a holy people, characterized as God's personal possession. The transformation of the people is indicated by their infusion of divine fear, which is a new, personal quality of character that emerges from the experience of hearing divine speech. This is a charismatic view of holiness, in which its transfer to humans is a divine gift (see the similar discussion by the apostle Paul in 1 Corinthians 13). It is the quality of divine fear, arising from the shared experience of holiness by the whole people of God, which provides the insight for the people to choose Moses as their representative to receive the additional words of God.

Moses represents the ideal of ordination to the divine word. He teaches the second generation that the divine word, now codified as the book of Deuteronomy, is the lifeline between the original events of salvation and their experience of them. The hearing of the divine word in scripture will keep the memory of the past event of the exodus alive for the second generation and for all subsequent generations, allowing holiness to invade the whole people of God through time. Moses repeatedly reminds the second generation that, in the very act of observing the written word of God, they are a "holy people."

The charismatic vision of holiness, as a gift that directly invades the whole people of God, is a radical view of the relationship between the sacred and the profane, which shares many characteristics with Otto's study of the numinous. The charismatic interpretation of holiness, moreover, gives rise to a functional understanding of ordination. The selection of Moses to the office of teacher and to the role of interceding for the community is not a contrast between a sacred clergy and a profane laity. Rather, the ordination to the word indicates a specific responsibility to ensure the continuing power of the divine word in the life of the people of God. The person ordained to the divine word is like an artist, who must both receive holiness in the form of the divine voice and also recreate it anew for the people of God, who, as we have seen, through their own infusion of holiness, are already art critics.

RESOURCES FOR FURTHER STUDY

Clements, R. E. *The Book of Deuteronomy: Introduction, Commentary, and Reflections.* Volume 2: *The New Interpreter's Bible.* Nashville, Tenn.: Abingdon, 1998.

Mayes, A. D. H. *Deuteronomy.* NCB. London: Oliphants, 1979.

Mettinger, T. N. D. "The Name Theology." In *The Dethronement of Sabaoth: Studies in the Shem and Kabod Theologies*, pp. 38–79. ConBOT 18. Translated by F. H. Cryer. Lund, Sweden: Gleerup, 1982.

Nelson, R. D. *Deuteronomy.* Louisville, Ky.: Westminster John Knox, 2002.

Olson, D. T. *Deuteronomy and the Death of Moses.* Minneapolis, Minn.: Augsburg Fortress, 1994.

Rad, G. von. *Deuteronomy.* Translated by D. Barton. Philadelphia: Westminster/ John Knox, 1966.

Terrien, S. *The Elusive Presence: Toward a New Biblical Theology.* New York: Harper and Row, 1978.

Weinfeld, M. *Deuteronomy and the Deuteronomic School.* Oxford: Clarendon, 1972.

Holiness and the Ordination to Sacramental Rituals in the Priestly Literature and in the New Testament

Moses functions as a mediator of holiness through rituals in the priestly literature. Our aim in this chapter is to describe the theology of holiness in the priestly literature in order to interpret the ordination to sacramental ritual that is modeled by Moses. We will also trace the same theology of holiness in selected New Testament literature. Jacob Milgrom's interpretation of holiness as a ritual resource will guide the study. The interpretation of Moses as the priestly mediator of sacramental rituals will require a broad study of the relationship of the sacred and the profane in the priestly literature. For this reason, the chapter will be separated into the following sections: The introduction will provide an overview of the literary design and the narrative context of the priestly literature in Exodus 19 through Numbers 10. "The Separate Quality of Holiness" will describe the way in which God is removed from the profane world. "The Sacred and the Profane" will change the focus from the separation of God and humans to the process by which holiness invades the profane world through the sacramental fire of the glory of Yahweh. The study of holiness and the glory of Yahweh will provide the background for an interpretation of "The Sacred and Ordination."

The Literary Setting of the Priestly Literature

The literary context of the priestly literature in Exodus 19 through Numbers 10 is important for interpreting holiness as a ritual resource and for understanding its implications for the ordination to the sacrament in

Christian tradition. The priestly teaching on holiness is concentrated in the events at Mount Sinai. The Israelites arrive at Mount Sinai in Exodus 19, and they do not depart from the mountain until Numbers 10. The central events at Mount Sinai include the progressive descent of the glory of Yahweh into the profane world (Ex 24, 40; Lv 9), the construction of the Tabernacle (Ex 25–40), the creation of the sacrificial rituals (Lv 1–7), the ordination of the priesthood to mediate the rituals (Lv 8–10), the rules of purity (Lv 11–16), the ethics of holiness (Lv 17–27), and the formation of a religious community around the sanctuary (Nm 1–10). This overview indicates that the priestly literature is not confined to a single book, as was the case with the teaching on holiness in Deuteronomy. In fact, the priestly teachings span the books of Genesis, Exodus, Leviticus, and Numbers. Although the events at Mount Sinai contain the most extensive teachings on holiness and ordination, the priestly account of creation in Genesis 1 also provides important information on the sacred and the profane, as we have already seen in the discussion of holiness in chapter 1.

The narrative context of the priestly literature in Exodus 19 through Numbers 10 creates a series of contrasts to the book of Deuteronomy. The account of the revelation at Mount Sinai describes the original event of the first generation of the Israelites, as compared to the book of Deuteronomy, where Moses recounted a past event of revelation at Mount Horeb to later generations. The setting of the revelation at Mount Sinai provides the initial clue that the problem of history and religious experience in the book of Deuteronomy will be addressed very differently when holiness is interpreted as a ritual resource, rather than as the dynamic voice of God recorded in scripture. The revelation at Mount Sinai suggests a more direct encounter with holiness for all future Israelites through sacramental rituals.

The narrative context of the priestly literature is accompanied by changes in literary style and in the role of Moses. The book of Deuteronomy is made up of sermons by Moses, in which he seeks to persuade the second generation of Israelites about the authenticity of the religious experience of their ancestors at Mount Horeb. The persuasive sermons of Moses aid the later generation in overcoming the distance between their present situation and the original experience of hearing the voice of God. Moses remains a central actor in the priestly account of the events at Mount Sinai, but his role changes from the persuasive speaker to the recipient of divine speech. God instructs Moses throughout Exodus 19 through Numbers 10 on the nature of holiness. The motif of holiness occurs nearly 250 times in the divine instructions.

The divine speeches in the priestly literature lack the rhetoric of persuasion in the book of Deuteronomy. They are delivered in a more formal, matter-of-fact style, which is characterized by an overabundance of detail. All aspects of the architectural design and the furnishings of the sanctuary are spelled out according to their material, composition, shape, and ability to transmit holiness. The same detailed precision dominates the instructions for the rituals of the sanctuary. The precise descriptions are required because the sanctuary, rather than the people of Israel, is the location of holiness. The focus on the sanctuary as sacred space results in a more detailed description of sacramental objects and rituals. The objective nature of the speech contrasts to the rhetoric of persuasion in the book of Deuteronomy, in which Moses sought to convince a later generation about the authenticity of past religious experiences.

The context and literary style of the priestly literature signal a very different teaching on holiness and ordination. The sanctuary and its furnishings become infused with holiness. The human encounter with holiness does not stem from a historical experience of the divine voice, which must be passed on to later generations. Rather, holiness becomes available in sacramental rituals, which allow for controlled access to sacred objects. As a result, holiness remains continually present for the people of God through the sacramental rituals of the Tabernacle.

This distinct interpretation of holiness changes the focus of worship practices. The emphasis in the priestly literature is no longer on religious experience and the power of human memory, which must be activated through the persuasive teaching of scripture. It is, rather, the need to provide safe access to sacred objects, which can harm as well as heal humans. Yahweh warns Moses at Mount Sinai: "Set limits around the mountain and keep it holy" (Ex 19:23). The apostle Paul provides a similar interpretation of holiness, as a ritual resource to be protected, when he warns the Corinthians of the danger of the Eucharist: "For all who eat and drink without discerning the body, eat and drink judgment against themselves" (1 Cor 11:29). The ordination of priests for the purpose of mediating the sacramental presence of God through ritual actions will play a prominent role in the priestly teaching on holiness.

The warning of the apostle Paul illustrates that holiness, as a ritual resource, is at the heart of the New Testament literature. The baptism of Jesus at the outset of his ministry and his final meal with the disciples at the conclusion of his mission remain continually present for Christians as a ritual resource through the sacraments of baptism and the Eucharist. The transfer of holiness in Christian sacraments is not rooted in the charismatic experience of the numinous, but in the act of participating in the rituals. The problem of history and religious experience fades when a person participates in the baptism of Jesus or feasts in the Eucharist with the risen Lord. Baruch A. Levine describes the immediacy of holiness as a ritual resource: "Whenever humans and God shared a sacred meal a bond was acknowledged to exist between them." Levine notes further that the sacramental presence of God in the sanctuary is especially true in Christian tradition: "Christianity adopted the policy of sanctifying space. . . . Christian worship in the form of the traditional mass affords the devout an experience of sacrifice, of communion, and proclaims that God is present. The Christian church, then, is a temple."[1]

The commission of Jesus to his disciples at the end of the Gospel of Matthew illustrates the important role of holiness as a ritual resource in the New Testament and its influence in the ordination to the sacrament in Christian tradition. The Gospel of Matthew concludes with the theme of memory. Jesus states to his disciples: "Remember, I am with you always, to the end of the age" (Mt 28:20). The need for memory is not to recall a past religious experience from the mission of Jesus. It is, rather, the recognition of the present reality of Jesus through the ritual of baptism: "Go therefore and make disciples of all nations, baptizing them in the name of the Father, and of the Son, and of the Holy Spirit" (Mt 28:19). The ritual of baptism dissolves the tension between history and religious experience, which is central to the ordination of the divine word in the book of Deuteronomy. Instead, the commission of Jesus calls the disciples to the priestly ordination associated more closely with sacramental rituals, since the rite of baptism becomes the vehicle by which Jesus will be continually present through time. We will see in chapter 6 that the New Testament does not describe the ordained as priests. Yet, the commission of Jesus in the Gospel of Matthew illustrates that the priestly ordination to sacramental ritual is central to the New Testament.

The Separate Quality of Holiness

God is transcendent in the priestly literature, even more so than in the book of Deuteronomy. In chapter 4, we saw that the liturgy of the tithe

(Dt 26:12–15) clearly separated God from the profane world of humans, when the worshiper declared the residency of Yahweh to be in heaven: "Look down from your holy habitation from heaven." The priestly literature separates God even further from the world of humans by including the region of heaven within the profane world. Genesis 1:1 states: "In the beginning God created the heavens and the earth."

Heaven is created in the priestly literature. It is neither the habitation of God nor is it holy. Heaven is part of the profane world in the priestly literature. It has a clear boundary, described as the "dome" (*raqia'*; Gen 1:8). Heaven has its own source of water, which is held in place with windows (Gn 7:11). It contains an array of created objects, including the stars, the sun, and the moon (Gn 1:14–17). The creation of heaven is no different than that of the earth. Both have a beginning point and a conclusion. The region of heaven begins on day two of creation, when God names the dome that separates water: "God called the dome, 'heaven'" (Gn 1:8). Genesis 2:1 states the completion: "The heavens and the earth were finished." Finally, both heaven and earth exhibit their own development, described as a genealogy or generation: "These are the generations of the heavens and the earth when they were created" (Gn 2:4). The creation story in Genesis 1 indicates that God does not dwell in heaven any more than God dwells on earth.

The priestly literature never tells us where God dwells. Yet, Exodus 25:8–9 suggests that God does have a residence someplace. In providing Moses with plans for the Tabernacle, God describes the sanctuary and its furnishings as a "pattern" (*tabnit*) that is shown (*mar'eh*) to Moses. The meaning of the text is difficult. The word *tabnit* translates as "form, structure, shape, figure, or pattern," while *mar'eh* indicates a "vision" or even the "form of an object." A *tabnit* describes the blueprints for the Jerusalem temple (1 Chr 28:11). It may even describe a replica of the temple (1 Chr 28:19). The language indicates that Moses receives the plans of the Tabernacle from God in the form of a blueprint. The meaning "pattern" suggests further that the blueprint may even be of God's permanent home and thus a copy of it. But the permanent dwelling of God resists a location. The deity has become so transcendent in the priestly literature that God cannot be equated with any geographical region of the cosmos.

The priestly literature advocates an extreme form of divine transcendence, in which the sacred and the profane are far removed from each other. God pronounces the profane world of Genesis 1 to be good, but it is not holy. This is true for the regions of both heaven and earth.

Heaven, with its objects (sun, moon, and stars) and creatures (birds), is declared to be good. The region of earth receives the same evaluation: Water, land, fish, sea monsters, plants, animals, and humans of the earth are all good. But neither heaven nor earth nor any of their objects or creatures is holy. Genesis 1 extends the separation between God and humans beyond the book of Deuteronomy to the point where humans cannot even address God in the holy habitation of heaven. Holiness is, rather, an abstract moment in time, when God rests on the seventh day after creating the profane world of heaven and earth (Gn 2:1–3). Even God's resting place, however, is not identified, depriving humans of any resource for imagining the holy habitation of God.

Humans become further separated from the sacred world of God with the shedding of blood. Blood outside of the human body is a virus, which enters the created world when Cain kills Abel, as we have already noted in chapter 2. Once the blood of Abel penetrates the ground, it becomes a pollutant, rather than the life force within his body. The pollution of blood creates a further separation, which is both environmental and biological, between God and humans in the priestly literature. Humans are not only mortal (profane), they are also diseased and violent (impure), living in a world of environmental pollution, which drives the holiness of God even further away from the profane world.

The polluted environment of the profane world also mutates humans over time. The priestly literature charts the degeneration of humans as a change in diet from being vegetarian in Genesis 1 to becoming carnivores after the flood in Genesis 9. God describes the diet of humans in the ideal world of Genesis 1: "See, I have given you every plant yielding seed that is upon the face of all the earth, and every tree with seed in its fruit; you shall have them for food" (Gn 1:29). There is no shedding of blood in this world, not even among animals: "And to every beast of the earth, and to every bird of the air, and to everything that creeps on the earth, everything that has the breath of life, I have given every green plant for food" (Gn 1:30). But, after the flood, God concedes that all living creatures will fear and dread humans, because "every moving thing that lives shall be food for [them]" (Gn 9:3). In the post-flood world, the violence associated with shedding blood has become a way of life, which even influences the diet of humans.

The separation between purity and impurity compounds the distance between God and humans and between the sacred and the profane. Purity represents life, health, wholeness, order, and peace in the profane world of Genesis 1, as compared to the impure world of death, disease, decay, disorder, and violence that infects creation and humans after the murder of Abel. In the post-flood world, holiness is not only separate from creation, it must also be quarantined from death (Nm 19), human disease (Lv 13–15), moral violence (Lv 19), and the carnivorous diet of humans (Lv 11). The two-part separation between the holiness of God and humans in the post-flood world makes any contact between them volatile and dangerous.

The transcendence of God is presupposed in the New Testament. As a result, the literature provides little direct reflection on the separation of God from the profane world. In fact, the thrust of the literature is in the reverse direction to describe how God has invaded the profane world through the person and work of Jesus. Passing comments, however, allow for a portrait of the transcendent God. We saw in chapter 4 that the synoptic Gospels portray God dwelling in heaven. Matthew, for example, repeatedly refers to God as the "Father in heaven" (e.g., Mt 5:43, 6:1). The phrase occurs infrequently in Mark (11:25), Luke (10:21), and John, where God is also described as the "Father in heaven," who is able to provide humans with the "bread of heaven" (Jn 6:31–33). The identity of God as the Father in heaven serves the same function as the references to heaven in the book of Deuteronomy, where God is also located in heaven, separating the deity from humans on the earth.

But there are also glimpses of the priestly view of divine transcendence, where the deity is even further removed from the profane world of humans. The prologue to the Gospel of John provides illustration. Although the theme of John 1 is the preexistent nature of Jesus as the Logos, the hymn also portrays God before the creation of the world. John 1:1–3 states that the Logos existed with God prior to the creation and that all subsequent acts of creation occur through the Logos, rather than directly through God. Thus, in this hymn, God is very removed from creation. The vast distance between God and creation is reminiscent of the priestly literature, where God is so transcendent that the deity is even removed from heaven.

The Sacred and the Profane

Yahweh remains transcendent in the priestly literature, never descending into the profane world. And this is also true of the divine creator in the

New Testament literature. The glory of Yahweh, an essential characteristic of the deity, does take up residency in the Tabernacle sanctuary,
providing the healing power of holiness to the Israelites through sacramental rituals. We will see that New Testament authors also follow the
model of the priestly literature by describing Jesus as the glory of God,
whose blood also transmits the healing power of holiness to humans
through sacramental rituals. Our interpretation of holiness as a ritual
resource will be separated into two sections: "Covenant and Divine
Memory" will explore the self-imposed obligations of the deity to rescue
the profane world from impurity. "The Glory of Yahweh at Mount
Sinai" will describe the process by which the sacred invades the profane
world.

Covenant and Divine Memory

The relationship between the sacred and the profane is grounded in a
theology of covenant in both the book of Deuteronomy and in the
priestly literature. The nature of covenant, however, is very different in
the priestly literature from that in the book of Deuteronomy, which, in
turn, changes the role of memory in the two traditions. The contrast
provides important background for distinguishing the ordination to the
divine word from the ordination to sacramental ritual.

Covenant makes the relationship between the deity and humans
possible in the book of Deuteronomy. The Israelites become a holy
people when they hear the voice of God at Mount Horeb, which results
in their choosing to enter into covenant with God. Thus, in the book of
Deuteronomy, covenant is dependent on the Israelite people. They must
choose the covenant and, once the choice is made, their behavior is
restricted by it. Moses tells the people in Deuteronomy 4:13: "He [God]
declared to you his covenant, which he charged you to observe." The
observance of covenant begins with the people's memory. Their rec-
ollection of the past revelation of law at Horeb is the basis for obedience.
The need for the Israelites to remember a past event defines the role of
Moses in the book of Deuteronomy. He is idealized as a persuasive and
charismatic speaker. Moses repeatedly encourages the people to remember the exodus, the sabbath, and especially the law (e.g., Dt 5:15;
7:18; 8:2, 18). Divine memory plays almost no role in the book of
Deuteronomy, appearing only once in Moses's intercession for forgiveness after the sin of the golden calf: "Remember your servants,

Abraham, Isaac, and Jacob; pay no attention to the stubbornness of this people" (Dt 9:27).

The responsibility for maintaining the covenant and the role of memory are reversed in the priestly literature. The restrictions associated with the covenant and the burden of memory rest with God in the priestly literature and not with humans. Covenant, moreover, is not dependent upon human choice, but upon the decision of God alone. The theme of covenant in the priestly literature is introduced at the close of the story of the flood in Genesis 9:8–17, when God states to Noah: "I now establish my covenant" (Gn 9:9). Covenant in the priestly literature is self-imposed by God: "I now establish." The content of the covenant is that "never again shall all flesh be cut off by the waters of the flood, and never again shall there be a flood to destroy the earth" (Gn 9:11). There are no conditions or time limits on the covenant. God states that it exists "for all future generations" (Gn 9:12).

The covenant in the priestly literature is a free action of God to restrict the divine use of destructive power against the profane world. Although the restriction is self-imposed, God loses freedom in making covenant. God gives up the power to destroy the impurity of the profane world through the flood. God states to Noah: "I will maintain my covenant" (Gn 9:11). God does not say that Noah must observe the covenant. In fact, the covenant does not require any particular observance by Noah. It only restricts God, especially in how the deity will exercise power in the profane world. The covenant with creation at the close of the flood forces God to nurture a relationship with the profane world while trying to purify it, even though impurity repels God. The deity will make a similar covenant with humans, when God states to Abraham in Genesis 17: "I will establish my covenant between me and you, and your offspring after you throughout their generations, for an everlasting covenant, to be God to you and to your offspring after you" (Gn 17:7).

The divinely self-imposed restrictions of covenant with creation and with Abraham put the burden of memory in the priestly literature on God and not on humans, as was the case in the book of Deuteronomy. In the priestly literature, God must continually remember the covenant and thus maintain a relationship between the sacred and the profane. Signs accompany the covenant in the priestly literature to remind God of his obligations. The rainbow is the sign of the covenant with creation (Gn 9), while circumcision is the sign with Abraham (Gn 17). The signs prompt

God, not the people, to remember the covenant. God states at the close of the flood: "I have set my bow in the clouds, and it shall be a sign of the covenant between me and the earth. When I bring clouds over the earth and the bow is seen in the clouds, I will remember my covenant . . . and the waters shall never again become a flood to destroy all flesh" (Gn 9:13–15). The speech underscores that it is God who must remember the covenant through time. In the same way, the covenant with Abraham places the obligation of memory on God, which is underscored when Yahweh states to Moses at the outset of the exodus: "I have heard the groaning of the Israelites whom the Egyptians are holding as slaves, and I have remembered my covenant" (Ex 6:5; see also 2:24–25).

The covenant and divine memory provide the basis for sacramental rituals in the priestly literature. One result of the performance of rituals is that God is reminded of past promises, allowing the power of holiness to be transmitted through the ritual. The bread of presence in the Tabernacle is a remembrance for Yahweh (Lv 24:7), as is the blowing of trumpets: "They shall serve as a reminder on your behalf before Yahweh your God" (Nm 10:10). The new covenant announced by Jesus also reflects the priestly interpretation of covenant and divine memory. God creates the new covenant in the body and blood of Jesus. The effectiveness of its power is not dependent upon human choice or memory. The Gospel of Matthew describes the cup of wine in the Eucharist as the divine decision for a new covenant: "For this is my blood of the covenant, which is poured out for many for the forgiveness of sins" (Mt 26:28). The apostle Paul extends the interpretation of the ritual cup to address the role of memory: "This cup is the new covenant in my blood. Do this, as often as you drink it, in remembrance of me [*eis tēn hemēn anamnēsin*]" (1 Cor 11:25). The liturgy may be calling the participants to remember Jesus through the sacrament. But it may also reflect the role of divine memory in the priestly literature, in which case, the ritual prompts God to remember the new covenant. The bread and wine are then signs to prompt God's memory, like the rainbow after the flood or circumcision with Abraham.

The interpretation of covenant and divine memory in the priestly literature changes the purpose of ordination. The ordination to the divine word in the book of Deuteronomy is functional. It originates from the choice of the people to have a representative to mediate divine speech. It continues in tradition to encourage the people to remember the events of salvation history, when they became a holy people, and to persuade them to observe the covenant, which they chose to enter. The ordination to sacramental ritual in the priestly literature indicates an office. It derives from the choice of God, not the people. The task of the priest is to prompt divine memory of the covenant and salvation through ritual actions. The stones in the breastplate of Aaron (Ex 28:12, 29; 39:7) and the leadership of priests in the liturgical festivals (Nm 10:10) are meant to arouse God's memory of covenantal promises of salvation. The divine memory is aroused when the priest approaches God through rituals, which ensures the healing power of holiness in the sacramental rites. The apostle Paul reflects the same priestly ordination to sacramental ritual in the mediation of the Eucharist when he states: "I received from the Lord what I also handed on to you" (1 Cor 11:23).

The Glory of Yahweh at Mount Sinai

Yahweh is unable to enter the profane world in the priestly literature. Exodus 19:20–24 states the reason in two divine speeches to Moses, when Yahweh warns Moses of the danger to the Israelite people of direct exposure to the deity. The descent of God into the midst of the Israelites would result in many people perishing. Exodus 24:15–18 tempers the danger of the sacred in the midst of the profane world, when the glory of Yahweh descends to the summit of Mount Sinai in place of the deity. The glory of Yahweh is not Yahweh, but represents the essential nature of God's holiness. The glory of Yahweh provides the counterpart to the name of God in the book of Deuteronomy. Both represent a qualified form of divine holiness in the sanctuary. The name of God represents the dynamic power of holiness, which is available to all Israelites through the persuasive teaching of scripture. The glory of Yahweh indicates the sacramental power of holiness, which is transmitted through cultic objects and rituals. The glory of Yahweh takes up residency in the Tabernacle sanctuary through a three-stage descent: (1) onto the summit of Mount Sinai (Ex 24:15–18); (2) into the Tabernacle sanctuary (Ex 40:34–38); and (3) into the altar (Lv 9:22–24). The descent of the glory of Yahweh provides the framework for interpreting the role of ordination to sacramental rituals in the priestly literature.

THE DESCENT TO THE SUMMIT OF MOUNT SINAI. Exodus 24:15–18 describes Moses at the summit of the mountain alone, when "the Glory of Yahweh settled on Mount Sinai, and the cloud covered it for six days;

on the seventh day he called to Moses out of the cloud" (Ex 24:16). The story underscores that "the appearance of the Glory of Yahweh was like a devouring fire on the top of the mountain in the sight of the people of Israel" (Ex 24:17). The descent of holiness into the profane world as the glory of Yahweh is not a voice which immediately penetrates all of the people. There is no sound at all. Instead, the people only glimpse the glory of Yahweh at an extreme distance. The distance between the people and the glory of Yahweh indicates that, unlike the revelation at Mount Horeb, the people do not become holy from the event at Mount Sinai. In fact, the priestly literature does not even state that Moses is holy.

THE DESCENT INTO THE TABERNACLE. Exodus 40:34–38 describes the further descent of the glory of Yahweh from the summit of Mount Sinai into the Tabernacle after the construction of the sanctuary in Exodus 35–39: "The Glory of Yahweh filled the Tabernacle" (Ex 40:34). The further descent of holiness into the profane world raises a new problem, however. How are the Israelites able to gain access to the healing power of holiness, when it is inaccessible? Even Moses is unable to enter the Tabernacle, suggesting that he, too, is incompatible with holiness: "Moses was not able to enter the Tent of Meeting because the cloud settled upon it, and the Glory of Yahweh filled the Tabernacle" (Ex 40:35). The book of Exodus ends with a problem. What good is the descent of holiness into the profane world, if humans are unable to access its healing power through sacramental rituals?

THE DESCENT INTO THE ALTAR. Leviticus 9:22–24 resolves the problem of holiness through the ordination of the priests in Leviticus 8–9. Once a process of ordination is established to purify Moses and the Aaronide priests, they are able to enter the Tabernacle: "Moses and Aaron entered the Tent of Meeting" (Lv 9:23). Thus, it is the ordination of priests that leads to a further descent of holiness into the profane world. The ritual actions of Moses and Aaron in blessing the people after the ordination of the priests orchestrates the further descent of holiness: "Moses and Aaron . . . then came out [of the Tabernacle] and blessed the people" (Lv 9:23). The priestly blessing transmits the healing power of holiness to the larger community, which prompts the glory of Yahweh to leave the confines of the Tabernacle and to enter the altar, bringing the holiness of Yahweh even closer to the people: "The Glory of Yahweh appeared to all the people. Fire came out from Yahweh and consumed the burnt offering and the fat on the altar, and when all the people saw it, they shouted and fell on their face" (Lv 9:23–24).

The Gospel of John reflects the pattern of the priestly literature. It also describes Jesus, the Logos (*logos*), as the glory (*doxa*) of God, who descends to earth and "tabernacles" (*skēneō*) with humans as a source of healing: "And the word [*logos*] became flesh and lived [*skēneō*] among us, and we have seen his glory [*doxa*], the glory [*doxa*] as of a father's only son, full of grace and truth" (Jn 1:14). The Logos and the glory of Yahweh are both essential characteristics of the deity, while also separate from God. The glory of Yahweh in Exodus 24:15–18 is not identical with the God Yahweh from Exodus 19:20–24. The same is true of the Logos. It shares in divinity ("the Logos was divine [*theos*]"), but exists separately from the God ("the Logos was with the God [*pros ton theon*]"). The wedding at Cana (Jn 2), the feeding of the five thousand (Jn 6), and the healing of the blind man with water (Jn 9) illustrate that the "tabernacling" presence of the Logos in the Gospel of John provides the healing power of holiness through rituals, as does the glory of Yahweh in the priestly literature.

The Sacred and Ordination

The glory of Yahweh, as a ritual resource for holiness, gives rise to the office of the ordination to sacramental rituals. The formation of the priestly office of ordination is tied closely to the construction of the Tabernacle sanctuary. The ritual actions in sanctuaries are intended to mediate the life force of holiness to humans. But sanctuaries and their sacramental rituals also require specialized personnel who are immunized to the dangers of holiness through the ordination to perform sacramental rituals—a process in which members of a select group become holy themselves, taking on the status of priests. Moses models the priestly ordination to perform sacramental rituals, which allows for the safe transfer of holiness to the people of God. Yet, as was evident already in the priestly call of Moses in Exodus 6–7, Aaron often assumes the central role in the description of the priestly ordination within the Mosaic office.

The Origin of the Ordination to Sacramental Rituals

The office of the priesthood is described in Exodus 28–30, and the ordination ritual is recounted in Leviticus 8–9. Exodus 28–30 is a divine revelation to Moses about Aaron and his sons. Leviticus 8–9 recounts the ordination ritual, in which Moses guides Aaron and his sons through the rite of passage from the profane world to take up service in the sacred realm of the sanctuary.

The selection of priests in Exodus 28 is objective, almost appearing to be arbitrary. God simply states to Moses: "Bring near . . . your brother Aaron, and his sons with him, from among the Israelites, to serve me as priest" (Ex 28:1). The call to priesthood does not include the introspection we associate with prophets or other charismatic religious leaders in the Bible. There is no give and take of an initial encounter with God, characterized by human objection and divine reassurance, as we see in the commissioning of prophets like Isaiah (Is 6) or Jeremiah (Jer 1). And, unlike the ordination to the divine word in the book of Deuteronomy, the people play no role in the priestly ordination to perform sacramental rituals. Instead, God elects persons to the priesthood (Nm 16:5, 17:20), suggesting that the call to the priesthood is institutional and objective. It is not based on a shared religious experience of the whole people of God.

THE SANCTUARY SETTING. The more objective and institutional nature of the ordination to sacramental ritual is illustrated by comparing it to the demand for a tithe in Leviticus 27:32: "All tithes of herd and flock, every tenth one that passes under the shepherd's staff will be holy [i.e., separated out] to Yahweh." The holy status of the tithe does not arise from any charisma of the chosen animal. Rather, in the act of separation, the animal leaves the possession of its human owner, enters the realm of God, and becomes a divine possession. And, as such, it is holy. The divine demand for a select group to become priests suggests the same process of transfer from the profane to the sacred realm. God requires a select group to mediate holiness in a safe manner, so that it heals rather than destroys humans. The priestly ordination to perform sacramental rituals, therefore, is more than a function of ministry; it is, rather, a distinct *office* that must be fulfilled. The office arises from the separation that is inherent in holiness and from the fact that the Israelite people do not, themselves, become holy. The personality or charisma of the priest will not provide the bridge between God and humans in fulfilling the priestly ordination to perform sacramental rituals. Rather, it is the ritual role of the priest in worship which overcomes the separation that is inherent in holiness. Thus, the power and authority of the priest resides in rituals, not in the charismatic power of the person to be a persuasive teacher.

The ordination of priests originates at Mount Sinai. The fear that Yahweh might descend into the midst of the people establishes the need for priests to work in the presence of God, to represent the people before God, and to mediate holiness to the people of God (Ex 19:20–24). In fact, the first reference to priests occurs in this episode. All of the tasks of the priests take place in the Tabernacle, which will require that they become holy in order to work in the sacred space of the sanctuary. But the holiness of priests does not result from a direct invasion of the spirit of God, as we often associate with more charismatic leaders and as voiced by the prophet in Isaiah 61:1: "The spirit of the Lord is upon me." Rather, holiness penetrates priests in a more objective manner through sacred rituals and vestments.

THE VESTMENTS OF ORDINATION. The objective character of the priestly office is underscored by the focus on clothing, rather than the person. Exodus 28:2 emphasizes that the office of priest is grounded in the divine demand to wear holy clothes: "You shall make sacred vestments [*bigdē-qōdesh*] for the glorious adornment of your brother Aaron." The garments will empower Aaron, transforming him into a priestly official. The command alerts us to the fact that the office of priest is inseparable from the vestments of the priesthood, as Jacob Milgrom underscored in chapter 2. The remainder of Exodus 28 describes in detail the clothing of the priestly office. And the ordination ceremony of the priests is largely a process of robing (Ex 29; Lv 8).

The focus on clothing underscores the central role of the priest to mediate holiness through rituals. The vestments serve to protect the priest in the presence of God, much like the gear of firefighters protects them from the heat of a blaze. The vestments will also transform the priest into a ritual celebrant who is capable of bridging the worlds of God and humans. In other words, the vestments and the priestly ordination are intertwined, underscoring once again that the power and authority of the priest in worship resides in the ritual, not in the person. Eleazar, Aaron's son and successor to the high priestly office, assumes his new office by putting on his father's vestments (Nm 20:28). We sometimes describe ordained clergy who lose their offices as being "defrocked," meaning "the removal of the monk's garment."

THE SEPARATE STATUS OF THE PRIEST. The priestly ordination to the sacrament is not simply an instance of "the clothes make the person."

Priests undergo a process of purification too, in which they not only put on holy clothing, but they themselves become holy (Ex 28; Lv 8). And by becoming holy, the priest is separated from the whole people of God, who are not themselves holy. This absence of holiness in the laity contrasts to the book of Deuteronomy, where all the Israelites hear the divine voice at Mount Horeb and become holy. The priestly view of holiness as a ritual resource concentrates holiness in the sanctuary and in the priests, who work within it. Korah, Dathan, and Abiram state the position of the book of Deuteronomy, when they confront the priestly ordination of Aaron and Moses: "All the congregation are holy, every one of them, and Yahweh is among them. So why then do you exalt yourselves above the assembly of Yahweh?" (Nm 16:3). In the priestly view, the claim that holiness resides in all of the people is a rejection of the sacramental presence of God in the sanctuary. The holiness within the sanctuary becomes a source of judgment, rather than healing, on the group. Yahweh kills the rebellious group for not acknowledging the sacred character of the sanctuary and the special status of the priests who work within it.

We often think of the separation between a holy priesthood and a profane laity as hierarchical and, as such, an instance of power and privilege. But biblical authors view the separation differently. The office of priest results in a loss of freedom for the sake of the larger community. Individual priests give up many of the freedoms of the profane world in order to be mediators for the whole people of God in the setting of the sanctuary. An important question for anyone pursuing the priestly ordination to the sacrament in Christian tradition is to determine what freedoms one is giving up or losing by becoming ordained. If candidates cannot think of any, they have not yet squarely confronted the priestly ordination to the sacrament.

When the office of priest is viewed as a privilege, it results in death to the priest, as is illustrated in the story of Aaron's two eldest sons, Nadab and Abihu (Lv 10:1–2). God kills them for offering "unholy fire" at the altar. The text is vague about their exact actions, but the rebuke of Moses to Aaron in verse 3 suggests that the two priests were viewing their office as one of privilege, rather than service. Moses conveys the following divine message to Aaron: "Through those who are near me I will show myself holy, and before all the people I will be glorified." The rebuke suggests that Nadab and Abihu were undertaking private forms of mediation, focusing on themselves instead of the people of God. Moses counters their private ritual with the command to Aaron that the office of the priest is meant to mediate holiness to "all the people." It is not meant to accentuate the privilege of a few. From this perspective, the hierarchy inherent in the ordination of priests, which arises from the very nature of holiness itself, is always inverted, meaning that the priestly ordination to the sacrament is to serve the whole people of God. The story of Jesus washing the feet of his disciples in John 13 captures the inverted hierarchy of the priestly ordination.

The Responsibilities of the Ordination to Sacramental Rituals

THE MEDIATION OF HOLINESS. The primary responsibility of the ordination to perform sacramental rituals is to mediate holiness between the sacred world of God and the profane world of humans. The sphere of the priestly ordination is restricted, for the most part, to the sanctuary. Ancient Israelite priests performed the task of mediation through cultic sacrifices, whose power was sacramental. The mediation of sacrifices purged humans, drawing them closer to the realm of God, now centered in the sanctuary. The whole burnt offering (*'olah*), the sin offering (*hatta't*), and the guilt offering (*'asham*) purged humans. The well-being offering (*shelamim*) even allowed Israelites to feast in the presence of God before the sanctuary. The mediation of the ordained priest was crucial for the ritual process to be effective. The sequence of the Tabernacle sacrifices represents a liturgical movement from sin and forgiveness to celebration, in which the priest functions as a religious health care professional, since the rituals allow for the divine medicine of holiness to be distributed to humans.

The ritual performance of baptism and the Eucharist also draws Christian clergy into the role of priestly mediation. In performing baptism, the minister, as priest, mediates the holiness of God, making the baptized person new in Christ, meaning that he or she is purged and now free from sin (*hatta't*) and guilt (*'asham*), while the ritual of the Eucharist transforms the well-being offering (*shelamim*) into a messianic banquet. The rituals of baptism and the Eucharist continue the priestly ordination to the sacrament in Christian tradition, since it is only through their proper performance that the holiness of God is transferred to the people of God. Christians overcome the pollution of death and violence as a result of the sacramental rituals, and they take on new lives in Christ.

THE ETHICAL DEMANDS OF HOLINESS. The aim of the priestly mediation is directed to the life of the laity in the profane world. Although
the laity do not achieve ritual holiness like the priests, the whole people of
God must seek to be holy through their actions: "You shall be holy, for
I am holy" (e.g., Lv 11:45). An additional aim of the ordination to
sacramental rituals is that the priests equip the Israelite laity to be ethical
agents for God in the profane world. The priestly mediation of holiness in
the sanctuary through rituals empowers the laity. The transfer of blessing
from God to the people of God is yet another means by which the laity
are empowered for their task. Aaron assumed this office when he blessed
the camp from the door of the sanctuary (Lv 9:22–24; Nm 6:21–26).
Blessing transmits the peace and the health of holiness to the people of
God. Aaron, as priest, placed the name of God upon the Israelites with
the words "Yahweh bless you and keep you; Yahweh make his face to
shine upon you, and be gracious to you; and Yahweh lift up his coun-
tenance upon you and give you peace" (Nm 6:22–26).

The blessing of Aaron indicates that the priestly vocation is not
confined to the ordained priesthood nor to the sacred rituals of the
sanctuary. Yahweh states a broader vision of the priestly vocation at
Mount Sinai. Yahweh intends for the whole people of God to "become a
priestly kingdom and a holy nation" (Ex 19:6).[2] The divine statement
clarifies that the goal is neither for holiness to remain confined in a
sanctuary nor that its transformative power be restricted to an ordained
class of priests. God desires all of the people of Israel to receive holiness
and to become holy themselves. The broader intention of God is reinforced with the additional divine proclamation: "All the earth is mine!"
(Ex 19:5). God's universal rule is the setting in which the holiness of the
nation is meant to function. The people of God must take on the role of
priests to the entire world.

The divine promise at Mount Sinai that the entire Israelite nation in
addition to the priesthood would become holy introduces gradations of
holiness at Mount Sinai in God's plan to reclaim a polluted and violent
world.[3] The gradations of holiness decrease in intensity from God to the
earthly sanctuary, where priests transfer holiness to the people through
sacramental rituals. The gradations of holiness continue further, however, from the priesthood and the sanctuary to the whole people of God.
The reason for this further progress is that holiness is too dynamic to
remain restricted to the sanctuary. All of the earth belongs to God. And
God desires that holiness move from the sanctuary to the world. It is not

the ordained priests who will fulfill this vision. It is, rather, the people of God, who receive holiness through worship, empowering them upon leaving the sanctuary to become mediators of holiness to the entire world. The priestly vocation in the world belongs to the laity, not the ordained. It is the Israelite people who must function as priests to the nations, extending the holiness of worship into the world at large (Is 61:5–6).

The proclamation of Jesus that "the time is fulfilled and the kingdom of God has come near" (Mk 1:15) is a message about the descent of holiness into our world.[4] The author of Hebrews interprets Jesus as mediating this holiness through his priestly vocation, as high priest (Heb 4–10). The priestly vocation of Jesus does not eliminate the vocation of priest, however. The apostles are baptized with fire (Acts 2) and commanded to perform sacramental rituals, especially baptism (Mt 28:16–20). The church will always need priests, who give up freedoms of the profane world in order to fill the office of mediation in worship. But the priestly vocation is not restricted to the ordained priest. When priests fulfill their role of mediation, holiness is unleashed through baptism into the life of the whole people of God. All Christians become infused with the Holy Spirit, bringing us one step closer to the divine vision in Exodus 19:5–6, that holiness influence the quality of life throughout the earth.

This is a grand vision of holiness, in which the sacramental life of worship is translated into an ethical mission to the world. It is a vision in which the priestly vocation of the ordained in the sanctuary and the priestly vocation of the laity in the world work in consort to fulfill the divine vision of a transformed earth. The author of 1 Peter captures the vision of the priestly vocation in the world. The author reminds baptized Christians that they are now a "royal priesthood" and a "holy nation" (1 Pt 2:9). The author provides guidelines for Christians to recognize the progression of holiness from the sanctuary into the larger world. We will know that holiness is infiltrating our larger world when we are purged of malice and envy (1 Pt 2), when we live and interact with others through love, not hate (1 Pt 3), and, especially, when we willingly absorb violence through suffering as an antidote to the contagion of sin (1 Pt 4).

ADDITIONAL RESPONSIBILITIES AND OFFICES OF ORDINATION. The role of priests, as mediators between the sacred and the profane, branches out to include a range of additional responsibilities. All administration of the sanctuary is part of the priestly ordination, including the upkeep of the cultic site and its finances (Nm 7–9). The priestly ordination also includes discernment. The discernment of the priest is the institutional insight about God's direction for the people of God. This role of institutional discernment is associated with the vestments of the priest, especially the breastplate and, more particularly, the *urim* and *thummim* worn by Aaron, with which he would seek judgments from God (Ex 28:15–30). Teaching is yet another responsibility of the priestly office and is also related to discernment. Moses tells Aaron that he must distinguish between the sacred and the profane and between the pure and the impure, and that he must teach these matters to the Israelites (Lv 10:10–11). Finally, discernment can even take on a more judicial role when the priest is required to determine the guilt or innocence of people's specific actions within the community of faith (Nm 5–6). All of these institutional forms of leadership, including administration, finance, teaching, and discernment, are aspects of the priestly ordination to the sacrament.

The priestly ordination also includes a variety of forms of health care, which are viewed as an extension of the sacramental power of God. Priests are to oversee the physical and spiritual health of the community as part of the blessing of the community noted above. In scripture, the priests evaluated illness (Lv 13) and judged whether a person was healthy (Lv 14). The important role of pastoral care and counseling, hospital visitation, and chaplaincy continues the priestly vocation of health care in the contemporary church. And, in this context, it is also a priestly responsibility to evaluate the ethical frontier of health care, where the church must clarify the meaning of life and death as our medical practices continue to change and evolve. The ethical reflection on life and death surrounding types of health care, euthanasia, stem-cell research, and abortion are priestly functions of discernment, which cannot be separated from the sacramental rituals of holiness.

The emphasis on holiness as a ritual resource within sacred space gives rise to clearly defined offices in the priestly ordination. The offices of ordination represent levels of holiness, which allow for different degrees of access to the sacramental presence of holiness within the sanctuary. The different priestly offices are represented through vestments. Three offices of ordination emerge in the priestly literature: the office of the high priest, the office of the priest, and the office of the Levite. The three offices provide a loose parallel to the Christian offices of bishop, presbyter, and deacon, in which the first two offices include the performance of sacramental rituals, while the last is one of service.

The high priest is the most holy office. The high priest is required to enter the holy of holies on the Day of Atonement to perform the ritual purification of the sanctuary (Lv 16). The vestments of the high priest reflect the holy status of the office. The vestments are described in Exodus 28:1–39. They include an ephod, breastplate, robe, checkered tunic, turban, and sash. The materials and colors are extravagant, including gold, blue, and purple cloth, crimson yarn, and fine linen. The complexity of the vestments and the extravagant material symbolize the close proximity to holiness, which characterizes the ritual role of the high priest. The ephod was likely an outer apron, in which were embedded stones with the names of the Israelite tribes. The stones functioned as a memorial for Yahweh to be mindful of the Israelite people. The "breastplate of judgment" was an additional vestment, which also functioned as a memorial for Yahweh of the Israelite people. Within the breastplate, the priest carried the *urim* and *thummim*, which may emphasize his role in discerning the will of God for the people. The high priest wore a blue robe underneath the breastplate, with pomegranates and bells on the hem. The bells were meant to protect the high priest upon entering the most holy place of the sanctuary. The high priest also wore special headgear, upon which was engraved "Holy to Yahweh." Finally, the high priest was also garbed with a tunic, turban, and sash.

The priests performed rituals at the altar of the sanctuary, which also required special vestments, which are described in Exodus 28:40–42. The ordination of the priests included their robing in a tunic, a sash, a headdress, and undergarments of linen. The headdress consisted of a cone-shaped turban. The linen undergarments may have been intended to prevent defilement. The purpose of the vestments was to glorify the office of the priest in the role of the ritual celebrant of holiness. Select priests were required to enter the sanctuary and care for the furnishings, but they were strictly commanded not to look upon the sacred objects, because of the danger of holiness (Nm 4:17–20).

The Levites were selected to serve the priests in caring for the sanctuary, although they were not allowed to perform sacramental rituals (Nm 8:23–26). In the role of service, the Levites represent the people of Israel as their substitutes in serving the sanctuary, and thus they atoned for the nation (Nm 3:44–51, 8:1–23). The Levites were not required to wear special vestments, although they and their clothes did undergo ritual cleansing.

Conclusion

The ordination to sacramental rituals in the priestly literature derives from the descent of the glory of Yahweh into the Tabernacle at Mount Sinai. The glory of Yahweh is idealized as fire, which invades the space of the Tabernacle, rather than the people of Israel. Thus, the sanctuary assumes the central role in this spatial interpretation of holiness. The transfer of holiness into the sanctuary creates a separate environment from the impure world of humans. Holiness, moreover, not only fills the space of the sanctuary, it adheres to objects within the sanctuary. The priestly literature describes the architecture and furnishings of the Tabernacle in lavish detail, because they participate in the holiness of God. The same interpretation of holiness as a ritual resource also informs the Christian sacraments of baptism and the Eucharist.

The sacramental view of holiness presupposes gradations of holiness based on the location of objects in the sanctuary. The altar area is more holy than the sanctuary where the laity sit, because it is the location of the sacramental objects and rituals. The Israelites do not become holy from the descent of the glory of Yahweh in the priestly literature, even when they see the fire of God at the summit of the mountain. They remain in the impure and profane world outside of the sanctuary. They require access to the sacred space of the Tabernacle to receive the benefits of holiness. Not even Moses is able to enter the sacred space of the Tabernacle once the glory of Yahweh dwells within it.

The Aaronide priests represent the ideal of ordination to perform sacramental rituals. They are elected by God to serve in the realm of the sacred. The people do not choose them, as was the case in the book of Deuteronomy. The priests become holy through the rite of ordination, which allows them to work in close proximity to the sacred. This quality of holiness separates the priests from lay Israelites. The priest provides the bridge between the sacred and the profane. Those who are ordained must represent the laity before God, prompting divine memory. The priests also mediate the healing power of holiness to the laity in a safe manner through sacramental rituals. The objective character of the priestly ordination is underscored by the focus on clothing in their rite of ordination. The vestments protect the priests in the presence of God, while also transforming them into ritual celebrants. Once clothed, the priest is able to represent the people, reminding God of his covenantal obligations toward creation and humans. At the same time, the priest is also able to transfer blessing to the laity through sacramental rituals of healing.

RESOURCES FOR FURTHER STUDY

Houtman, C. *Exodus*. Volume 3: *Historical Commentary on the Old Testament*. Kampen, Netherlands: Kok, 1993.

Jensen, P. P. *Graded Holiness: A Key to the Priestly Conception of the World*. Sheffield, England: Sheffield Academic, 1992.

Levine, B. A. *The JPS Torah Commentary: Leviticus: The Traditional Hebrew Text with the New JPS Translation*. Philadelphia: Jewish Publication Society, 1989.

Mettinger, T. N. D. "The Kabod Theology." In *The Dethronement of Sabaoth: Studies in the Shem and Kabod Theologies*, pp. 80–115. Lund, Sweden: Gleerup, 1982.

Milgrom, J. *Leviticus 1–16*. AB 3A. Garden City, N.Y.: Doubleday, 1991.

Nelson, R. D. *Raising Up a Faithful Priest: Community and Priesthood in Biblical Theology*. Louisville, Ky.: Westminster/John Knox, 1993.

Wenham, G. J. *The Book of Leviticus: The New International Commentary on the Old Testament*. Grand Rapids, Mich.: Eerdmans, 1979.

CHAPTER SIX

Holiness and Ordination in the New Testament Literature

The theology of holiness and ordination in the book of Deuteronomy and in the priestly literature provides the foundation for the ordination to the word and the sacrament in Christian tradition. We have seen that the two theories of holiness, as a dynamic power and as a ritual resource, create the Mosaic office of ordination in Torah, in which Moses functions both as the charismatic teacher of the divine word and as the priestly mediator of sacramental rituals. Both aspects of the Mosaic office allow for the transfer of holiness through worship, which empowers the people of God to be ethical agents in the profane world. We have also seen that the two theories of holiness influence the New Testament literature. Jesus is both the word made flesh and the sacramental glory of God, tabernacling with humans.

Yet, when the New Testament is interpreted as a resource for a theology of holiness and ordination, it presents a series of challenges. The literature contains a rich variety of teachings on holiness, some of which we have noted in the previous chapters. But the New Testament contains only minimal and sporadic reflection on ordination. The reason is that the New Testament focuses nearly exclusively on the invasion of the sacred into the profane world through the mission of Jesus, leaving only glimpses of how the ordained mediate holiness as a consequence of Jesus. The imbalance raises questions about the role of the ordained in Christian tradition, at least as it is envisioned in the New Testament.

There is an additional problem with the New Testament literature in developing a theology of ordination. The aim of the New Testament authors is to describe the effect of Jesus' mission on all humans, which further subordinates a theology of ordination within the literature. The holiness of all Christians is underscored by the identification "saints" (*hoi hagioi*), meaning "holy ones" (e.g., Phil 1:1). The Gospel of John goes further in its imagery, describing Christians as "children of God" (Jn 1:13). A central theme in the book of Acts is that the infusion of the Holy Spirit is not reserved for the original disciples of Jesus (Acts 2:8), but is poured out on all Christians (e.g., Acts 2:8, 33, 38; 8:15; 10:44; 19:2), thus narrowing the distinction between the twelve and all other Christians. The "priesthood of all believers" in 1 Peter 2:9 blurs the distinction between clergy and laity even further, at least in its modern interpretation within Protestantism. The priestly office, moreover, is restricted to the mission of Jesus in the New Testament (the book of Hebrews) and absent altogether in the description of the ordained.

The language of holiness alone, however, is deceptive in the study and interpretation of ordination in the New Testament, because the separate role of the ordained *is* maintained in the literature. The central position of apostle (*hoi apostoloi*), in particular, suggests that the office of the ordained continues in the wake of the mission of Jesus. The intensity with which Paul argues for his apostolic status reinforces the role of ordination in the early church. Other, less developed offices of ordination are also noted in the New Testament, including deacon (*diakonos*), presbyter or elder (*presbutēros*), and bishop (*episkopos*).

Our goal in this chapter is to describe briefly the dynamic relationship between the sacred and ordination in the New Testament literature. The chapter will be limited to the offices of ordination just noted. Our study will underscore that the New Testament authors do not provide a fully developed theology of ordination for the emerging Christian church. The references to the ordained presuppose the more extensive theological reflection on holiness and ordination within the Mosaic office from the Pentateuch for background and, thus, require a broad view of biblical authority, in which the primary teaching on ordination remains in the Hebrew scripture, rather than in the New Testament. We will also see that a contemporary theology of ordination requires the subsequent theological reflection of the church to interpret the offices of apostle, bishop, elder, and deacon within specific denominations. The dynamic character of holiness and ordination in the ongoing life of the church will require the reader to pursue the official documents of ordination within his or her respective church, since the ordination to the word and sacrament takes on many different forms in Christian tradition.

The Apostolic Office

The most prominent office of ordination in the New Testament is that of
the apostle. The noun *apostle* is used eighty times in the New Testament,
and the more abstract noun *apostleship* also occurs infrequently (Acts 1:25;
Rom 1:5; and 1 Cor 9:2;). The noun apostle is infrequent in Mark (two
occurrences, 3:14; 6:30), Matthew (one occurrence, 10:2), and John (one
occurrence, 13:16), but is a central motif in Luke and Acts (thirty-four
occurrences). The noun is also prominent in the Pauline and pseudo-
Pauline letters (thirty-three occurrences). The word occurs an additional
eight times in the remainder of the New Testament literature (Hebrews,
Peter, Jude, and Revelation). Since the discussion of the office of the
apostle is concentrated in Luke, Acts, and the Pauline letters, these bodies
of literature will be the focus of our study.

The history of the apostolic office is not altogether clear from the
literature. The word apostle means "messenger" (*apostolos*) from the verb
"to send out" (*apostellō*). In the Hebrew Bible, the messenger of God
could be a divine or human figure who represented the deity. The
messenger of God appears to Hagar in the wilderness (Gn 16) and leads
the Israelites through the Red Sea (Ex 13–14). In these instances, the
messenger is a divine figure. But the messenger of God could also be a
human figure. The promised messenger to lead the Israelites toward the
promised land (Ex 23, 33), for example, may be Moses. Prophets are also
commissioned in the Hebrew Bible through the action of being sent out
(e.g., Is 6; Jer 1). They, too, are messengers of God.

The designation of an apostle is restricted in the New Testament, for
the most part, to humans. Only once is the term apostle used to describe a
divine messenger. The author of Hebrews describes the risen Jesus as
both an apostle and a high priest (Heb 3:1). The identity of human
apostles appears to lack clear definition in the earliest references within
the New Testament, when it is used to describe persons who are sent out
to represent the church (e.g., 2 Cor 8:23; Phil 2:25). It is not clear, in these
instances, whether the term actually defines a specific group of persons or
even an office. In the formation of the New Testament, however, the
term apostle is used in a more restricted way to describe a specific office of
ordination within the early church. But, even with the more restricted
use, debate continues over the process and nature of the apostolic office.
The office of the apostle is defined differently in Luke and Acts than in
the Pauline letters. We will see that the debate is based on the divergent

theories of holiness as a dynamic power and as a ritual resource, which also inform the Mosaic office in Torah.

The very existence of the office of the apostle indicates that the early church envisioned levels of holiness within the body of Christ, even though the entire people of God was considered to be sacred (i.e., saints). In 1 Corinthians 12, Paul describes a wide range of spiritual gifts that are bestowed on Christians, which, upon first reading, appears to play down a distinction between laity and the ordained. Yet, at the close of the chapter, Paul outlines the gradations of holiness among the people of God (1 Cor 12:27–30). He affirms the holy status of all Christians, stating: "You are the body of Christ and individually members of it." But he also indicates the separation between clergy and laity. He notes a range of offices within the church, of which the apostle is the most sacred: "And God has appointed in the church first apostles" (1 Cor 12:28).

The Apostolic Office as a Ritual Resource in Luke and Acts

The apostolic office in Luke and Acts conforms in many ways to the priestly ordination to sacramental rituals, which was described in chapter 5. The apostles are not chosen on the basis of their charismatic experience. Rather, they are simply elected by Jesus from the larger group of his disciples without a clear reason. The result of their election is that the apostles become mediators of holiness through ritual actions. We will interpret the origin of the apostles in the Gospel of Luke and the emergence of the apostolic office in the book of Acts.

THE ORIGIN OF THE APOSTLES. The apostles in the Gospel of Luke are restricted to the twelve persons who lived with Jesus. Thus, the origin of the designation of the apostles is historical for Luke. The twelve apostles walked with, talked with, ate with, and lived in close proximity to Jesus. The selection of the specific twelve apostles from Jesus' larger group of disciples is attributed wholly to the election of Jesus, and not to any particular charismatic quality of the twelve. Luke 6:12–13 simply states: "[Jesus] spent the night in prayer to God. And when day came, he called his disciples and chose twelve of them." The office of apostle, like the office of the priest in the Pentateuch, results from a divine election.

The twelve apostles are singled out in the Gospel of Luke in a number of different ways. They live with the historical Jesus (Lk 6:13–16). They are given power directly from the historical Jesus to cure disease. The power to heal is described as having authority over demons (Lk 9:1–10). The twelve apostles participate in the last supper with Jesus, during the week of his passion (Lk 22:14). Thus, they experience the original ritual of the Eucharist. The apostles are also witnesses of the resurrection of Jesus (Lk 24:10). And they are taught directly by the risen Jesus through the power of the Holy Spirit (Acts 1:2).

THE APOSTOLIC OFFICE. The selection of the twelve apostles in the ministry of Jesus is transformed into the apostolic office in the book of Acts. Acts 1:26 signals the shift in the understanding of an apostle from the twelve who lived with Jesus to an office of the church, when it employs the noun apostleship (*apostolēs*) to describe "an office of ministry" (*topon tēs diakonias*). The number twelve is significant to this office. It must be maintained even with the departure of Judas. The criteria for the replacement of an apostle are historical. The apostles must fulfill the requirements of having lived with Jesus and of having witnessed his resurrection. The selection, moreover, is similar to the election of the original twelve. The process is not based on a numinous experience, but on the casting of lots.

The apostolic office continues the power of the historical Jesus in the life of the church. The apostles are filled with the power of the Holy Spirit (Acts 2). The imagery of Pentecost is charismatic, especially when the disciples teach in multiple languages. The description of the event, however, is closer to the fiery descent of the glory of Yahweh in the priestly literature. The interpretation of the apostolic office in Luke and Acts confirms its close relationship to the priestly ordination to sacramental ritual. The experience of Pentecost transfers the apostles from the profane world into the realm of the sacred. Peter speaks for the apostles when he declares: "We obey God rather than human authority" (Acts 5:29).

The apostolic office represents the emerging institutional church in one location, Jerusalem (Acts 8). The apostles have the administrative responsibility for the church. They oversee the distribution of money (Acts 4:32–37). The apostles carry on the power of the historical Jesus by demonstrating signs and wonders (Acts 5:12). They teach converts (Acts 2:37–43), they testify to the resurrection (Acts 4:32–37), and they are ritual celebrants in the breaking of bread (Acts 2:37–43). The apostolic office also adjudicates questions of ritual purity, cultic membership, and lesser offices of leadership. Acts 15 describes the central role of the apostles in determining the importance of circumcision for achieving ritual purity. Acts 10 recounts the role of Peter in evaluating non-Jewish membership in the church. Acts 6 narrates the ritual power of the apostles to ordain deacons through the laying on of hands (Acts 6:6).

The power of the apostles as mediators of holiness through ritual is underscored in Acts 8:14–24. The story recounts the conversion and baptism of the Samaritans. Yet, the transfer of the Holy Spirit to the Samaritans requires the ritual actions of the apostles: "Peter and John laid their hands on them, and they received the Holy Spirit" (Acts 8:17). The transfer of holiness in this story is not a dynamic invasion of the numinous. Holiness is, rather, a ritual resource, which requires the laying on of hands. It is so physical and concrete that Simon wishes to purchase the power: "Give me also this power so that anyone on whom I lay my hands may receive the Holy Spirit" (Acts 8:19).

The holiness of God in Luke and Acts is a ritual resource in the life of the church, which is concentrated in the apostolic office. The office is narrowly defined in the Gospel of Luke. It is restricted to the twelve, whose election originates with Jesus. The selection of the twelve disciples is not a charismatic experience of the numinous. It is, rather, a random choice of Jesus. They receive power directly from Jesus to heal. They participate in the important events of Jesus' life, from his baptism to the last supper. They are also taught directly by the risen Jesus. As a consequence, the power of the risen Jesus is channeled through the apostles, which gives rise to the apostolic office. The Holy Spirit is certainly not confined to the apostolic office. In fact, the power of the Holy Spirit frequently surprises the apostles. Yet, the apostles must confirm the power of the Holy Spirit, often through the ritual means of the laying on of hands.

The Apostolic Office as a Dynamic Power in the Pauline Epistles

Paul acknowledges the apostolic office of the twelve, which is described in Luke and Acts. He notes their authority in the book of Galatians (1:17–19). But Paul also claims the calling to the apostolic office, even though he does not fulfill the requirement of having lived with the historical Jesus. Paul's claim to the apostolic office derives from his distinctive view of holiness as a dynamic power that has invaded him directly, rather than as the ritual resource of holiness that is passed on by touch through the followers of Jesus. We will examine both the origin of Paul's apostolic calling and its responsibilities.

THE CALL OF PAUL. Paul repeatedly claims the ordination to the apostolic office (e.g., Rom 1:1–5; 1 Cor 1:1; 2 Cor 1:1). A brief overview of the Pauline letters suggests that his claim to the apostolic office emerges as his ministry develops. For example, Paul does not claim the apostolic office in his first letter to the Thessalonians. But the letter to the Galatians begins with the self-identification: "Paul an apostle" (Gal 1:1). The accompanying description in Galatians 1:1 indicates the polemical background of his claim: The apostolic office for Paul is neither a "human commission" nor does it derive from "human authority." It rests solely on the power of "Jesus Christ and God the Father, who raised him from the dead." The polemical character of Paul's claim to the apostolic office arises from the fact that he did not know the historical Jesus, and thus, he does not fulfill the requirements of the office as they are outlined in Luke and Acts.

Paul roots his apostolic calling in a dynamic encounter with the risen Christ, in which holiness is transferred to him directly through a divine invasion. Paul refers to his life-changing epiphany in Galatians 1:15–17 as a numinous experience of holiness: "But when God, who had set me apart before I was born and called me through his grace, was pleased to reveal his Son to Me . . . I did not confer with any human being." The event is described in more detail in Acts 9. A flash of light confronts Paul, here named Saul, as he travels on the road to Damascus. Yet, his experience of the risen Christ is not visual, but a voice from heaven: "Saul, Saul, why do you persecute me?" The narrator confirms the auditory experience, stating that those around Saul saw no form, but only heard the sound of the voice. The imagery is reminiscent of the account of theophany in the book of Deuteronomy, where the numinous voice of God invades the Israelite people directly as a dynamic power at Mount Horeb; they too hear a voice, but see no form.

Paul claims his calling to the apostolic office on the basis of his numinous experience. He states to the Corinthians: "Am I not free? Am I not an apostle? Have I not seen Jesus our Lord?" (1 Cor 9:1). He elaborates on his apostolic calling later in the letter, stating that the risen Christ appeared to Cephas, the twelve, the five hundred, James, and all of the apostles: "Last of all, as to one untimely born, he appeared also to me. For I am the least of the apostles, unfit to be called an apostle, because I persecuted the church of God" (1 Cor 15:8–9). Thus, the authority of

Paul as an apostle does not derive from his having lived with the historical Jesus, but from his having encountered the voice of the risen Christ in a numinous event.

PAUL'S APOSTOLIC REPONSIBILITY. The important role of holiness as a dynamic power changes the nature and the goals of the apostolic office for Paul. The confirmation of the apostolic office in Luke and Acts was based on history and tradition. The twelve were required to have lived with Jesus and to have witnessed the resurrection. The responsibilities of the twelve were cultic and institutional, resembling the priestly ordination to sacramental ritual. Paul narrows the criterion of the apostolic office to an experience of the risen Christ, not the historical Jesus. He also changes the office to represent more the ordination to the divine word. The goal of Paul's ordination is to proclaim the gospel to the Gentiles (Gal 1:16). Paul even identifies himself as the "apostle to the Gentiles" (Rom 11:13).

Paul also changes the nature of the apostolic office. In claiming the apostolic office, Paul shifts the confirmation of his ordination from a divine election, which is made evident to the church through the casting of lots (Acts 1), to more charismatic criteria. He reminds the Corinthians: "The signs of a true apostle were performed" among them with patience. These signs included wonders and mighty works (2 Cor 12:12). The statement indicates that a calling must be confirmed by the laity, which is a view of ordination that is very similar to that of the book of Deuteronomy. The parallels to the book of Deuteronomy continue, when Paul authenticates his apostolic office charismatically in the success of his mission to the Gentiles, which he defines as his primary responsibility. He states to the Corinthians: "Are you not my work in the Lord? If I am not an apostle to others, at least I am to you; for you are the seal of my apostleship" (1 Cor 9:1–2). The apostolic office for Paul is an ordination to the divine word, in which he proclaims the gospel to the Gentiles. The authenticity of his ordination is evident in his success, not in the more traditional criterion of his having lived with the historical Jesus.

The Office of the Presbyter

The New Testament literature describes the office of the presbyter, which is often translated as "elder" from the Greek *presbuteros* (presbyter).

We will use the words "presbyter" and "elder" interchangeably. The word *presbutēros* occurs sixty-seven times in the New Testament. The word occurs twenty-five times in the Gospels to describe an office of leadership in second temple Judaism, where the elders are often presented as leaders along with the chief priests and the scribes. The book of Acts indicates a change in the use of the word from the Gospels. The office of the Jewish elders continues in the book of Acts (seven occurrences), but the book also introduces the office of the presbyter/elder as a leader in the Christian church (ten occurrences). The Pauline letters contain no reference to the office of the elder, suggesting perhaps the later formation of this office in the early church. The pastoral Epistles refer to the office of the elder (1 Tm 5; Ti 1), as do the books of James (5:14) and 1 Peter (5:1) and the letters of John (2 Jn 1:1; 3 Jn 1:1). The book of Revelation repeatedly describes twenty-four elders who sit around the throne of God (Rv 4:4–10, 5:5–14, 7:11–13, 11:16, 14:3, 19:4), which may also be a reference to a specific office in the early church.

The meaning and the distribution of the word *elder* allow for several initial conclusions, which will provide a point of departure for our interpretation of the office of the presbyter. First, nearly half of the occurrences of the word elder in the New Testament refer to "the tradition of the elders" in Judaism and the office of leadership that is associated with it. As a result, we will begin our study with a brief summary of the office of the elder in the Hebrew Bible, since this office may be influencing New Testament authors. Second, the absence of any reference in the Gospels to the office of the presbyter alerts us to the fact that, unlike the apostolic office, the New Testament writers did not feel the need to authenticate the office of the presbyter within the story of the historical Jesus.

The Tradition of the Elders in Second Temple Judaism

The role of the elders as representatives and as leaders in Israel is likely ancient, although the origin of such an office cannot be recovered with certainty. Historians assume that the elders played a leadership role in the earliest stages of ancient Israelite society as heads of clans or families (e.g., 1 Sm 11:13), regions (1 Sm 30:26), and perhaps even tribes (1 Sm 11:10). The elders would have played an active role in adjudicating local disputes, and they may also have assumed cultic responsibility in the gathered assembly.

The office of the elder emerges as an important leadership body in the post-exilic or second temple period. Jewish self-government under Persian rule consisted of two distinct leadership groups: the council of elders and the priests. The council of elders was likely made up of lay members, described variously as "prominent nobles" (e.g., Neh 2:16, 4:8), "elders of Judah" (e.g., Ezr 5:5, 6:7), and "heads of the fathers' houses" (e.g., Ezr 2:68, 4:2; Neh 8:13, 11:13). The titles indicate that the council of the elders provided a form of leadership distinct from that of the priests in Jewish self-government during the second temple period. Many of the descriptions of the elders in the Pentateuch likely reflect the role of the council of elders during this period, even though some of the stories may contain older traditional material. A summary of the role of elders in Exodus, Numbers, and Deuteronomy will provide background for interpreting the office of presbyter in the New Testament.

The elders are already singled out as leaders in the call of Moses in Exodus 3. Yahweh states to Moses: "Go and assemble the elders of Israel" (Ex 3:16). Thus, they emerge immediately in the book of Exodus as the leaders of the people, who must accompany Moses to Pharaoh to demand the release of the people from their slave labor (Ex 3:18). The elders return in a cultic role of leadership in Exodus 18 and 24, when they participate in the sacrifices with Jethro (Ex 18:12) and with Moses and Aaron on the mountain of God (Ex 24:9–11). The separate references to the elders and to the priests in Exodus 24 suggest the existence of two distinct offices.

The origin of the office of the elder is narrated in Numbers 11. The story begins when Moses complains to God that he is not able to lead the Israelite people alone: "I am not able to carry all this people alone, for they are too heavy for me" (Nm 11:14). The complaint repeats the theme from Exodus 18, when Jethro also advised Moses that he could not lead the people alone. God responds to Moses's complaint by creating a new office of leadership for seventy elders. The authority of the office originates in a charismatic and numinous experience, reminiscent of the theophany on Mount Horeb in the book of Deuteronomy. Moses leads the elders to the door of the tent of meeting, which is the name of the sanctuary in the book of Deuteronomy. God transfers a portion of Moses's spirit directly to the seventy elders, who become inspired momentarily with prophetic power: "Then Yahweh came down in the cloud and spoke to him [Moses] and took some of the spirit that was on him and put it on the seventy elders; and when the spirit rested upon them, they prophesied" (Nm 11:25). The office of the elder is not that of a prophet, however. Numbers 11:25 ends with the statement: "But they [the seventy elders] did not do so [prophesy] again." Instead, God describes the responsibility of the elders to be scribes, suggesting the responsibility to teach scripture (Nm 11:16), and to bear the burden of the people, suggesting some form of judicial oversight and administration (Nm 11:17).

The book of Deuteronomy provides a broad portrait of the office of the elder. The elders are singled out during the experience of theophany on Mount Horeb as the group that approaches to hear the words of God (Dt 5:23). The elders have liturgical responsibilities. They represent the people in the liturgy of the covenant (Dt 29:10). They also hear the words of the law and take on the responsibility of the covenant curses, if the people break their treaty with God (Dt 31:28). The liturgical role of the elders also leads to their responsibility to teach the law to the people (Dt 31:9). Finally, the elders also have administrative tasks, especially in judging the Israelites. The elders evaluate instances of murder, and they perform rituals to combat pollution that may result from unsolved murders (Dt 21:1–9). They also adjudicate family (Dt 21:18–21) and marriage (virginity, Dt 21:13–19; Levirate law, Dt 25:5–10) disputes. The portrait of the elders suggests that their office is more like the ordination to the divine word than like the ordination to sacramental rituals.

The Office of the Elder in the New Testament

The office of the elder is introduced abruptly in the book of Acts, as a distinct position from that of the apostles. There is no account of the origin of the office, as is the case with the apostolic office or with the office of the deacon. Instead, elders are simply acknowledged for the first time in Acts 11:30 to be the leaders of the churches in Antioch and Jerusalem, who oversee the exchange of the gifts for the Jerusalem church. The elders are associated with the apostles in Acts 15 in adjudicating the role of circumcision for maintaining purity in the early church, where their role is legal: The elders receive the legal matter; they review it with the apostles; and they respond with an official letter. Finally, elders are also described as the overseers of the church at Ephesus in Acts 20.

The office of the elder also occurs in late New Testament literature, where the office becomes more blurred with that of the apostolic office.

James 5:14 may retain a distinction between the office of elder and the apostolic office. The letter indicates that elders took on a special role of intercessory prayer and healing through the ritual of anointing. Yet, as we have seen, the ritual of healing is closely associated with the apostolic office. First Timothy and Titus provide a more detailed description of the office of elder. First Timothy 5:17–22 describes the responsibilities of the elder to administrate, preach, teach, and perform the ritual of laying on of hands, which is restricted to the apostolic office in the book of Acts. The elder is a paid position in 1 Timothy. Titus 1:5 adds that an elder must be blameless, married only once, with children who are professed Christians. First Peter and the letters of John blur the office of the elder and the apostolic office by identifying the author of the books as both an apostle (Peter in 1 Pt 5:1 and John in 2 Jn 1:1, 3 Jn 1:1) and an elder. The book of Revelation may also merge the two offices, when it describes the twenty-four elders who sit around the throne of God. If the image is a reference to the twelve tribes of Israel and the twelve apostles, then the elders have become the apostles in the book of Revelation.

Our brief summary indicates that there is no account of the origin of the office of the elder. In the book of Acts, the elders are simply introduced as leaders in the church. Their office is distributed broadly throughout the geographical reach of the early church. They are leaders of local congregations, described as shepherds. The pseudo-Pauline letters provide a more detailed portrait of elders as teachers, preachers, and administrators of local churches. Our interpretation of the elder in the New Testament also has required that we compare and contrast it to the more historically grounded apostolic office. The book of Acts distinguishes between elders and apostles. It portrays the elders as participants in larger judicial decisions, where they function along with the apostles. First Peter and the letters of John suggest less distinction between the two offices in the late first and second centuries, when the apostles Peter and John are also described as elders. The relationship of the office of the presbyter and the apostolic office remains unclear from the New Testament literature.

The Office of the Deacon

The New Testament describes the office of the deacon by employing the Greek word *diakonia*, which means "service." The verb *diakoneō* means "to wait at table" in the Greek world. The saying of Jesus in Luke 17:8 illustrates the primary meaning: "Would you not rather say to him, 'Prepare supper for me, put on your apron and serve [*diakonei*] me while I eat and drink.' " The imagery of waiting at table indicates that the office of the deacon is rooted in service which is rendered to another. Service is an ideal throughout the Gospels. The teaching of Jesus in Mark 9:35 is an example: "He [Jesus] sat down, called the twelve, and said to them, 'Whoever wants to be first must be last of all and servant [*diakonos*] of all' " (see also Mt 20:26, 23:11; Jn 12:26).

The origin of the office of the deacon is often associated with the selection of seven persons to serve food to the widows who were being neglected in Acts 6. In this story, the twelve apostles state: "It is not right that we should neglect the word of God in order to wait on tables [*diakonein trapezais*]" (Acts 6:2). The result is that seven persons are selected for the task and installed in the position through the ritual of prayer and the laying on of hands. It is doubtful, however, that this story represents the origin of the office of the deacon, since the seven persons are never described as "deacons."

The apostle Paul indicates that the office of the deacon was established already during his ministry. He opens the letter to the Philippians with the greeting: "Paul and Timothy, servants [*douloi*] of Christ Jesus; to all the saints in Christ Jesus who are in Philippi with the bishops [*episkopois*] and the deacons [*diakonois*]" (Phil 1:1). Paul's self-identification is that of slave (*doulos*). The greeting indicates that the entire church is composed of saints. They are led by persons in two distinct offices, bishops and deacons. In addition, Paul may also refer to the office of the deacon in his reference to Phoebe in Romans 16:1: "I commend to you our sister Phoebe, a deacon of the church at Cenchreae." The responsibilities of the deacons, however, are not clearly defined by Paul. The purpose of the letter to the Philippians is to thank the church for material gifts. The reference to the deacons in the greeting may highlight their role in the distribution of the gifts. Phoebe is also described as a benefactor in Romans 16:1, again suggesting the service of gifts.

The office of the deacon is described in the most detail in 1 Timothy 3:8–13. The office includes both men and women. Deacons should not be double-tongued. They should only be modest drinkers of wine and not greedy for money. Deacons must be established in the faith. They should be tested before they take office. They can only be married once with a well-established household.

The Office of the Bishop

The office of the bishop is perhaps the least developed in the New Testament. The noun *episkopos* occurs only five times. The verb *episkopeō* means "to visit, to watch over, to care for." The exhortation to the elders in 1 Peter 5:1–2 illustrates the meaning of the verb: "I exhort the elders among you to tend the flock of God that is in your charge, exercising the oversight [*episkopountes*] not under compulsion but willingly." In 1 Peter, the elders have the responsible of oversight, which suggests that there may have been overlap between the offices of the elder and of the bishop in the New Testament. Paul's letter to the Ephesian elders in Acts 20 illustrates further the mixing of the two titles. Acts 20:28 states to the elders: "Keep watch over yourselves and over all the flock, of which the Holy Spirit has made you overseers ["bishops"; *episkopous*]." Titus 1:5–7 continues the intermingling of the two offices. The passage is meant to provide direction for the appointment of elders in every town within Crete (Ti 1:5). In listing the qualifications of the elders, the author also describes their office as that of bishop (*episkopon*): "For a bishop as God's steward, must be blameless" (Ti 1:7–8).

The distinct office of the bishop is acknowledged by Paul in Philippians 1:1, where it is separated from the office of the deacon: "The saints in Christ Jesus who are in Philippi" are led by both bishops (*episkopois*) and deacons (*diakonois*) (Phil 1:1). The nature of the office, however, is not defined. The office of the bishop is described in 1 Timothy 3:1–7. It is a noble task, requiring persons above reproach, married only once, hospitable, and good teachers. The task of management and administration is highlighted, since the office requires that the person "take care of God's church."

The office of bishop is clearly established, however, in early literature of the church as a significant position of ordination. In *The Apostolic Tradition*, which may represent the earliest record of ordination practices in the church, perhaps dating from the early to mid-third century C.E., Hippolytus of Rome indicates the primary position of the office of bishop as distinct from that of elder (presbyter) and deacon. The people choose bishops, according to Hippolytus, but only bishops perform the rite of ordination, in the presence of elders, who observe the ceremony without participating. One bishop ordains elders, in conjunction with other elders, who also participate in the laying on of hands. Only one bishop participates in the ordination of a deacon, since the office of deacon is not an ordination to the priesthood, but a service to the bishop. The offices of ordination in Hippolytus are very similar to the three offices of ordination in the priestly literature, where the offices of high priest and priest are associated with sacramental rituals, while the office of Levite is one of service to the priesthood.[1]

Conclusion

We have seen that the New Testament literature contains an emerging theology of ordination. The conclusion of the Faith and Order Commission of the World Council of Churches on "The Forms of the Ordained Ministry" is helpful at this point: "The New Testament does not describe a single pattern of ministry which might serve as a blueprint or continuing norm for all future ministry in the church. In the New Testament there appears rather a variety of forms which existed at different places and times."[2]

The most developed office of ordination in the New Testament is the apostolic office. The theological reflection on the apostolic office embraces the two theories of holiness from the Mosaic office in the Pentateuch. Luke and Acts anchor the apostolic office as a ritual resource of holiness, which is transmitted through the twelve apostles who were elected by the historical Jesus. Paul's claim to the apostolic office is based on an interpretation of holiness as a dynamic force in his life, which invaded him through a theophany of the divine word on the road to Damascus. The New Testament indicates a tension between the two interpretations of the apostolic office, which remains unresolved in the literature in the same way that the priestly and prophetic aspects of the Mosaic office are also not harmonized in Torah.

The distinctive offices of ordination and their relationship to one another are not clarified in the New Testament. We have seen ambiguity between the apostolic office and the office of the presbyter especially in the late literature in the New Testament. The ambiguity between the office of the presbyter and the bishop is even more pronounced. Most of the references to the office of the bishop in the New Testament occur in the larger context of stories about the office of the presbyter. *The Apostolic Tradition* of Hippolytus, which dates from the early to the mid-third century C.E., indicates a clearly developed threefold office of ordination including bishop, elder, and deacon.

This brief overview of the offices of ordination in the New Testament underscores the need for a broad view of biblical authority, in which the teachings on ordination in the Hebrew scriptures provide the framework for theological reflection. Thus, it is the Mosaic office in Torah that provides the most detailed guidelines on the ordination to word and sacrament in Christian tradition. But scripture alone is inadequate for constructing a contemporary theology of holiness and ordination. *The Apostolic Tradition* of Hippolytus indicates that the identity of clergy (*kleros*), meaning those who are set apart by lot to serve the sacred, also requires the postbiblical theological reflection of the church universal and the more specific guidelines of individual denominations.

RESOURCES FOR FURTHER STUDY

Albertz, R. *A History of Israelite Religion in the Old Testament Period.* Volumes 1 and 2. Translated by J. Bowden. Louisville, Ky.: Westminster/John Knox, 1994.

Betts, H. D. "Apostle." In *The Anchor Bible Dictionary.* Volume 3, edited by D. N. Freedman, pp. 309–11. Garden City, N.Y.: Doubleday, 1992.

Countryman, L. W. *The Language of Ordination: Ministry in an Ecumenical Context.* Philadelphia: Trinity Press International, 1992.

Hippolytus, Antipope, *On the Apostolic Tradition.* English version with introduction and commentary by Alistair Stewart-Sykes. Crestwood, NY: St. Vladimir's Seminary Press, 2002.

Küng, H. (ed.). *Ecumenical Theology: Apostolic Succession: Rethinking a Barrier to Unity.* Concilium 34. New York: Paulist Press, 1968.

Schmithals, W. *The Office of the Apostle.* Translated by J. E. Stelle. Nashville, Tenn.: Abingdon, 1969.

Stewart-Sykes, A. *On the Apostolic Tradition: Hippolytus.* Crestwood, N.Y.: St. Vladimir's Seminary Press, 2002.

Warkentin, M. *Ordination: A Biblical-Historical View.* Eugene, Ore.: Wipf and Stock, 1982.

CHAPTER SEVEN

The Mosaic Office and the Ordination to Word and Sacrament in Christian Tradition

The final chapter of our study has three related goals. One goal is to fashion a biblical theology of ordination which is grounded in the complex nature of the Mosaic office. Such a theology must be canonical in scope. It must maintain the distinctive prophetic and priestly characters of the Mosaic office, while also relating the two characteristics to a comprehensive biblical theology of ordination to word and sacrament in Christian tradition. A second goal is to explore how the structure of the Mosaic office provides the foundation for ordination to word and sacrament in Christian tradition. A third goal will be to describe how individual communities relate to the prophetic and the priestly dimensions of the Mosaic office in unique ways, which gives rise to the rich variety of forms of ordination in Christian tradition. We will also see that the variety of possible relationships between the prophetic and priestly aspects of the Mosaic office far exceeds the interpretation of any one denomination. The result is that the Mosaic office provides both the resource for the formation of clergy within individual faith communities and the basis for a broad ecumenical biblical theology of ordination.

The Ordination to the Mosaic Office

The study of the Mosaic office in Torah has underscored that ordination has social, liturgical, and organizational implications. But these aspects of ordination do not probe the central nature of the Mosaic office. Ordination to the Mosaic office emerges from broad theories of holiness, which include comprehensive world views about the separation of the sacred and the profane, the danger of the sacred to the profane world, and how these distinct realms may be safely bridged by God and by humans. We have seen that interpreters explore the nature of the separation of the sacred and the profane in a variety of ways. Mircea Eliade described two modes of experience to distinguish the sacred from the profane.[1] Rudolf Otto characterized the sacred as the wholly other, which is infused with the dynamic power of the numinous.[2] Jacob Milgrom preferred the more spatially oriented imagery of separation to describe holiness as that which is withdrawn from the common.[3] All of the authors agree that holiness creates separation between the sacred and the profane. The biblical authors accentuate the separateness of holiness by describing it as a quality that emanates from the character of God, even though it cannot be equated directly with the deity. The incompatibility of the sacred and the profane and the need for profane humans to participate in the power of the sacred gives rise to the vocation of ordination.

The Sacred, the Profane, and the Rite of Passage of Ordination

The primary responsibility of the profession of ordination is to serve the sacred in order to mediate holiness to other humans.[4] The mediation of holiness may be through sacramental rituals, intercessory prayers, or charismatic interpretations of the divine word. Whatever the means of the mediation of holiness, sanctuaries are the principal work setting for the ordained. We have seen that the Latin *ordinare* points to the central role of the sanctuary, since the term describes a select group of humans who give up the freedom of the profane world in order "to put in order, arrange, and prepare" the sacred world of the sanctuary for the mediation of holiness through worship. The setting of the sanctuary underscores the divine origin and authority for the profession of ordination, as compared to the secular setting of power in the profane world. Yet, we also have seen that holiness is a dynamic power, which cannot be contained within sanctuaries. As a result, holiness seeks to invade the profane world outside of the sanctuary. The dynamic character of holiness influences the profession of ordination, since it directs worship within the sanctuary to an ethical mission of health and justice in the profane world. In this way, the work of the ordained in the sanctuary is never detached from the mission of the whole people of God in the world.

The role of the ordained to serve the sacred indicates that the process of ordination requires a rite of passage in which candidates undergo transition from the profane world to the sacred. Arnold van Gennep describes the structure of the rite of passage as consisting of three phases: the act of separation from a social structure; the transitional stage when a person is outside of the recognized social structure; and the re-incorporation of the person into the new world.[5] The ordained are separated from the profane world through the process of ordination. Candidates enter a period of transition, which removes them from the social structures of the profane world and prepares them to serve the sacred within the sanctuary.

Moses models the rite of passage in the process of ordination, where the focus remains on the liminal or transitional stage. The biblical authors reject the heroic model of leadership which dominates in the profane world. The profession of ordination is not a rags-to-riches story which idealizes the natural leadership abilities of its members. Moses fails as a heroic profane leader when he kills an Egyptian in secret to rescue the Israelites from oppression. This action eventually leads to Moses's flight from Egypt to save his life from the death threat of Pharaoh. Moses's rite of passage to ordination moves in a different direction. It includes the breakdown of his sense of self-power and security, which opens him to new experiences of the sacred beyond the boundaries of his own self-will and sense of power. The result is that the ego of Moses becomes transparent, allowing him to mediate holiness through his person, which sets him on the path of ordination.

The biblical authors use the setting of the wilderness to symbolize Moses's religious rite of passage. The rite of passage to ordination begins with Moses's initial confrontation with holiness in the burning bush, and it continues until his face is permanently transformed by the invasion of divine light. Three aspects of ordination emerge from the story of Moses's rite of passage. First, the shining skin of Moses signifies that ordination is service to the sacred, which requires transition from the profane world of humans to the sacred realm of God. Second, the ignorance of Moses about his transformation indicates that the authority of ordination resides in an act of God and not in a human decision. Third, the fact that the divine light never leaves the face of Moses, requiring that he wear a veil outside of worship, indicates both the permanence and the liminal nature of the profession of ordination. Service to the sacred is not a nine-to-five job. Dennis M. Campbell captures the message of the biblical author in the story of Moses's shining face when he states: "Referring to the ordained minister as a profession involves the recognition that there is a pastoral character and identity which transcends any specific work, and involves a person's total life, not just one's 'occupation.'"[6]

The Two Theories of Holiness and the Ordination to Divine Word and Sacramental Rituals

We have seen that two theories of holiness, as a dynamic force and as a ritual resource, influence the Mosaic office in Torah and the apostolic office in the New Testament. Rudolf Otto described one theory of holiness as the numinous, which he characterized as a dynamic force that invades humans directly as a spiritual gift.[7] Humans experience the charismatic gift of the numinous as an awakening to the mystery and fascination of holiness. The reception of the numinous through religious feeling and the loss of the ego through the sense of creature-consciousness are necessary for any person seeking the prophetic ordination to the word in Christian tradition. The power of holiness resides in the relationship between God and the one who is called out. This special relationship is the source for a functional role of the ordained within the prophetic ordination to the divine word. The ordination occurs when the people of God recognize the charisma of the leader, whose ego has become transparent through the encounter with the numinous power of holiness, allowing God to speak through him or her. As Max Weber concluded, such personal power sets a person apart as one endowed with exceptional qualities for authoritative leadership.[8]

Moses models the charismatic office of prophetic ordination in his encounter with holiness in the burning bush and in his role as a charismatic teacher of the divine word in the book of Deuteronomy. The apostle Paul extends the model into the New Testament, when the risen Christ unexpectedly confronts him on the road to Damascus, which leads to his apostolic ordination and mission to the Gentile world. Both Moses and Paul receive an infusion of holiness, which propels them on the journey of their call experience and eventual ordination. Each actor emerges as a charismatic teacher of God's dynamic power, which was revealed in a past event of salvation history. In the book of Deuteronomy, Moses teaches the second generation of Israelites about their parents' firsthand experience of the exodus. Paul conveys the power of the risen Christ to Gentiles, who are also removed from any experience of the historical Jesus. Thus, the charismatic ordination of both men addresses the problem of religious experience in a historical context. The ordination to the divine word addresses the problem of history and religious experience through the prophetic interpretation of past tradition accompanied by persuasive speech about its significance for later generations. The interpretation of scripture and the preaching of the divine word in Christian worship continue the prophetic ordination of Moses and Paul into the religious experience of present worshiping communities.

Jacob Milgrom described another theory of holiness, as a ritual resource which is performed in sanctuaries.[9] Milgrom emphasized the spatial character of the separation of holiness and its concentration in the sanctuary through the definition of holiness as that which is withdrawn from common use, be it a temple building or precinct, or the objects and persons within the sanctuary. Milgrom challenged the judgment that rituals within the sanctuary represent a mechanical and uninspired form of religion. He argued instead that the mediation of holiness through sacred rituals represents an active and dynamic power, which enters the world through the sacred location of a sanctuary, while also seeking to transfer its power to the profane world in order to combat impurity.

The priestly ordination is essential for the safe transfer of holiness through sacramental rituals and for the ethical mission of the sacred in the profane world. The priestly ordination is not grounded in the immediate and personal invasion of the numinous, which requires extensive self-criticism of the religious experience, nor is the power of holiness in the personal relationship between God and the ordained. Rather, candidates for the priestly ordination undergo critical training in tradition in order to pass institutional standards, which are necessary to become ritual celebrants within the sanctuary. The power of holiness in the priestly ordination, therefore, is in the status of the priest as one who is equipped to approach the sacred for the sake of the whole people of God. The sacred status does not arise from the personal charisma of the priest, nor from a special relationship between the priest and God. Rather, the special status of the priest is objective and institutional, which is represented most clearly through the prominent role of vestments in the ritual of ordination. The ordination of the priest through rituals of purification, touch (the laying on of hands), and clothing allows the ordained to come into close proximity to sacred objects and to mediate the healing quality of holiness through rituals. The prominent role of vestments indicates that the ability of the priest to mediate ritual holiness arises solely from the priestly office and not from the charisma of the priest. Thus, the priestly ordination to sacramental ritual represents a change of status in the ordained. The priestly office of ordination allows the priest to mediate sacred rituals for the whole people of God.

Moses models the priestly office of ordination in the priestly literature. His call to ordination in Exodus 6–7 is neither a charismatic invasion nor an introspective religious experience. The priestly call of Moses is more external and public in nature. The call originates in the divine memory of past covenantal promises, which results in Moses's public election to the priestly office at a time of crisis. The setting of the call in Egypt, rather than in the isolation of the wilderness, reinforces the public nature of the office. Moses is commissioned to mediate the plagues into the land of Egypt, which will force Pharaoh and the Egyptians to acknowledge Yahweh. The priestly ordination in Exodus and Leviticus continues the focus on the ritual mediation of holiness, when Moses directs the construction of the Tabernacle and fashions the sacrificial rituals, which allow the sacramental presence of the glory of Yahweh to descend into the altar.

The apostles in Luke and Acts also reflect the priestly ordination of Moses. In the Gospel of Luke, the apostles too receive their office from a divine election, which lacks the introspection of Paul's encounter with the risen Christ on the road to Damascus. The apostolic office in the book of Acts further develops the institutional focus of the priestly ordination. When a new apostle must be chosen after the death of Judas, the criteria are based on tradition and the noncharismatic action of casting lots. The authority of the apostles in the book of Acts is also institutional and priestly. It is most evident in their ability to transfer holiness through the ritual action of healing, to maintain purity, and to oversee ordination through the laying on of hands.

The priestly ordination of Moses and the apostles in Luke and Acts bridges the problem of history and religious experience in a decidedly different manner than the ordination of Moses in the book of Deuteronomy and the apostle Paul's encounter with the risen Christ in the New Testament. In Deuteronomy and in the apostolic ordination of Paul charismatic teaching was necessary to prompt human memory of the past events of salvation. The priestly ordination with its focus on rituals activates the divine memory of past promises of salvation, which occasions the transfer of holiness through sacraments. The ritual transfer of holiness in the priestly ordination provides a continual, direct, and immediate encounter with the primary events of salvation history. Thus, the transfer of holiness through sacramental rituals extends the past events of salvation into the present life of the people of God. The immediacy of holiness through sacramental rituals defines the priestly office of ordination, since in mediating sacramental rituals, the priest not only transfers holiness to the people, he or she also represents the people before God.

The Call to Ordination

The Mosaic office emphasizes the need for a call experience as part of the process of ordination. Moses's call to ordination requires a rite of passage, in which he undergoes transformation from a hero in the profane world to a religious leader who serves the sacred. We have seen that biblical authors identify two distinct types of call experience, which correspond to the two theories of holiness as a dynamic force and as a ritual resource. Moses is first invaded by holiness as fire in the wilderness experience of the call, before he undergoes a more institutional experience of the call in the land of Egypt. A brief summary of the two experiences of holiness in Moses's rite of passage will clarify how the same processes continue to inform the call experience of candidates for the ordination to word and sacrament in the Christian tradition.

The wilderness call of Moses arises from the charismatic experience of holiness as a dynamic power. It gives rise to an introspective experience of holiness, which probes the inner life, testing the ego of Moses through self-examination. The prophetic call is personal and filled with self-doubts, which are reflected in the dialogue between Moses and Yahweh. The introspective and dialogical process draws out the deity to clarify the nature of holiness as a charismatic gift and as a resource for Moses to persuade the elders of the authenticity of his prophetic call to ordination.

The institutional call of Moses probes the ritual power of holiness within tradition. This experience of holiness is more public in nature. It probes the authenticity and the suitability of Moses's call experience within the context of tradition. The rite of passage requires that Moses acquire the knowledge and skill to become a ritual specialist who is able to mediate holiness in a variety of public and liturgical settings, both to the Egyptians and to the Israelites. Mastery of the sacramental resources of holiness clarifies the power of God in past tradition as background for understanding the priestly call in the present time, which leads to the insight that the traditional God, El Shaddai, is now appearing to Moses with the new name of Yahweh during the Israelites' crisis in Egypt.

The two experiences of holiness work in tandem throughout Moses's liminal period of discernment in the rite of passage of ordination. Candidates for ordained ministry at my institution identify with both of the call experiences of Moses as part of their rites of passage. Many describe personal encounters with holiness which mirror the characteristics of Moses's wilderness call, including the sudden invasion of holiness, the resistance to the commission, the divine reassurance of the authenticity of the experience, and the breakdown of the ego through testing in order to become a transparent voice for God. Other candidates root their call experiences institutionally in the ritual transfer of holiness through baptism, which is less about the introspection of the ego and more about locating the candidates' call to ordination within a broad priestly genealogy of past and present leaders, in order to clarify the challenges to the church at this juncture in history and tradition.

The literary settings of the two calls of Moses suggest that the two experiences function together in discerning the call to ordination, rather than functioning in separation as though they represented competing views of ordination. The goal for discerning the call to ordination is to uncover the power of holiness in both the wilderness and the institutional call experiences. Candidates who overly emphasize the charismatic experience of holiness fail to see the formative role of institutional training in history and liturgy in the rite of passage of ordination. In these cases, seminary education or the judicatory formation of candidacy become little more than hoops through which they must jump to become ordained, since the one-sided focus of such candidates leads them to believe that their ordinations were already authenticated in their private experiences of holiness as the numinous. Candidates who focus only on the institutional mastery of history, liturgy, and rituals risk losing the inspiration and the development of character that emerges from the charismatic experience of holiness. Both the wilderness and the institutional experiences of the call are formative in the rite of passage to Christian ordination. The order of the distinctive experiences of holiness is unpredictable and unimportant. For Moses, the charismatic invasion of holiness preceded his priestly call, while for Jesus the ritual transfer of holiness through baptism provided the occasion for his subsequent testing and critical self-reflection in the wilderness. In each case, the biblical authors underscore that the whole experience of holiness, as dynamic power and as ritual resource, is greater than the sum of the parts in the rite of passage of ordination.

The Identity of the Ordained

Our study of the Mosaic office allows for three conclusions, which shape the identity of the ordained and give direction to the Christian profession of ordination to word and sacrament. First, the Mosaic office grounds the profession of ordination in the whole people of God. It is the cry of Israel that prompts the commission of Moses in both the prophetic and priestly calls to ordination. The second conclusion moves in the opposite direction, namely, that the ordained are distinct from the whole people of God. Moses's rite of passage of ordination is first and foremost for the purpose of serving the sacred, not humans. It is only through his separation from the profane world in service of the sacred that Moses is able to lead the whole people of God. Third, the Mosaic office embodies prophetic and priestly dimensions, which can neither be harmonized nor separated from each other. The dynamic tension between the prophetic and the priestly aspects of the Mosaic office gives definition to the Christian profession of ordination to the word and sacrament. Each of these insights requires further elaboration.

First, the profession of ordained ministry is grounded in the religious vocation of the whole people of God. *The Faith and Order Paper on Baptism, Eucharist, and Ministry* by the World Council of Churches underscores the organic connection between the ordained and the life and mission of all Christians by structuring its conclusions on ordination into three related sections, which progress from "The Call of the Whole People of God" to the more focused reflection on "The Church and the Ordained Ministry" and "The Forms of the Ordained Ministry."[10] Stephen V. Sprinkle summarizes well the intent of the *Faith and Order* statement when he concludes: "As a rite of the church, ordination affirms the call of God to the whole community of faith."[11] H. Richard Niebuhr cements the organic relationship between the ordained and the church universal when he describes four distinct pastoral vocations, of which the first is "the call to be a Christian."[12] All Christians share this calling with the ordained, and it is not possible to be ordained without this foundational call. As a result, ordained ministry is never the possession of an individual or a select group, nor can it be given away by an individual. It is always corporate, public, and attached to the whole people of God. William H. Willimon captures the organic relationship between church and the ordained when he concludes that ordained ministry is multi-vocal, including both a divine voice and the voice of the church.[13] *The Faith and Order Paper on Baptism, Eucharist, and Ministry* summarizes well the unity of the ordained and the whole people of God: "The ordained ministry has no existence apart from the community. Ordained ministers can fulfill their calling only in and for the community. They cannot dispense with the recognition, the support and the encouragement of the community."[14]

The organic relationship between the ordained and the whole people of God is essential in the development of the Mosaic office. As we have noted, both the priestly and the prophetic commissions of Moses originate in the cry of the Israelites. God declares to Moses in the prophetic commission: "The cry of the Israelites has come to me; I have also seen how the Egyptians oppress them. So come, I will send you to Pharaoh to bring my people, the Israelites, out of Egypt" (Ex 3:9–10). The same words repeat in the priestly commission, when Yahweh states: "I have also heard the groaning of the Israelites whom the Egyptians are holding as slaves, and I have remembered my covenant" (Ex 6:5). The commissions of Moses are corporate, public, and attached to the whole people of God.

The close relationship between the ordained and the whole people of God continues in the descriptions of leadership in Deuteronomy and in the priestly literature. The authority of Moses as the charismatic teacher of the divine word in Deuteronomy emerges organically from the shared experience of holiness, in which all of the Israelites hear the voice of God at Mount Horeb. The divine execution of Aaron's two sons Nadab and Abihu for undertaking private forms of mediation also reinforces the close ties between the ritual mediation of holiness and the whole people of God in the priestly literature. Moses's rebuke of Aaron bonds the priestly rituals with the people: "This is what Yahweh meant when he said, 'Through those who are near to me I will show myself holy, and before all the people I will be glorified'" (Lv 10:3). Moses himself undergoes a divine rebuke, when he separates his office from the Israelite people at the close of the wilderness journey and acts independently in wrongly accusing the people of being rebels, when they request water in the desert (Nm 20:1–13). The divine judgment on Moses's abuse of office is swift: "Because you did not trust in me, to show my holiness before the eyes of the Israelites, therefore you shall not bring this assembly into the land that I have given them" (Nm 20:12). The Mosaic office in both its prophetic and priestly roles models the organic relationship between the ordained and the whole people of God.

Second, the call to ordination results in a separate profession from the call of the whole people of God. *The Faith and Order Paper on Baptism, Eucharist, and Ministry* notes that "the church has never been without persons holding specific authority and responsibility" to proclaim the word of God, to celebrate the sacraments, and to guide the life of the community of faith in worship, mission, and in its caring ministry."[15] The responsibilities of the ordained underscore the central role of the sanctuary as the location where clergy fulfill their vocation. The danger of abuse of power is ever present in the separation of a professional clergy. For this reason, current literature on ordination often emphasizes the service nature of leadership in the office of ordination, in order to ground the vocation of the ordained in the life of the whole people of God.[16] The emphasis on servant/leadership accentuates an essential characteristic of the Mosaic office, but it does not penetrate to the core of ordination, with its grounding in holiness. Ordination which is not grounded first in holiness is doomed to produce a profession that lacks identity and purpose.

Our study of the Mosaic office has clarified that holiness inevitably introduces separation between the profane and the sacred worlds. This is evident in the description of the Israelites. They are separated out as "holy people" in the book of Deuteronomy and as "a kingdom of priests" in the priestly literature, which underscores the religious vocation of the whole people of God. The ordination of Moses as prophet and as priest introduces a further separation between him and the Israelites for the purpose of mediating the life-giving power of holiness to the whole people of God through worship. Moses is separated from the people to convey the voice of God to Israel in Deuteronomy and to transmit holiness through rituals in the priestly literature. The shining face of Moses and his need to wear a veil outside of the sanctuary underscore his permanent separation from the Israelites as a result of his ordination.

The Mosaic office underscores that the mediation of holiness is only possible through a rite of passage in which Moses first serves the sacred. The message of the Mosaic office is that, without distinguishing ordination as a separate profession, the mediation of holiness to the whole people of God will be weakened. An emphasis on servant/leadership without first grounding such leadership in holiness blurs the identity of clergy, who then run the risk, according to Henri J. M. Nouwen, of becoming "pseudo-psychologists, pseudo-sociologists, [and] pseudo-social workers." Such persons are enablers, facilitators, and even role models, but such acts of service have little to do with ordained leadership.[17] Niebuhr underscores the separate profession of the ordained by identifying a series of unique call experiences beyond the call to be a Christian, which is shared by the whole people of God. He describes the rite of passage into the profession of ordained ministry as including the secret call, which is reminiscent of Moses's prophetic call in the wilderness; the providential call, which embraces the training for office in the priestly call; and the ecclesiastical call, which results in the rite of ordination.

Third, the Mosaic office embodies prophetic and priestly dimensions, which can neither be harmonized nor separated from each other. The dynamic tension between the prophetic and the priestly aspects of the Mosaic office gives definition to the Christian profession of ordination to the word and sacrament. Stephen V. Sprinkle describes the nature and identity of ordained ministry as arising from a series of five tensions, which probe the nature of the separation between the ordained and the whole people of God: first, the one and the many; second, ordination as a functional or sacramental profession; third, ordination as a priestly office or a charismatic gift; fourth, the ordained as ambassadors and mediators for God or as suffering servants for the whole people of God; and fifth, whether the act of ordination is a rite or a process. How one answers the five points of tension will define the nature of ordination and the identity of the ordained.[18] Sprinkle concludes that, rather "than requiring one view to prevail and another to fail," the "opposite poles establish tensions that may be held together creatively."[19]

The Mosaic office, with its prophetic and priestly aspects of ordination, embodies the full range of tensions described by Sprinkle. Both the prophetic and the priestly ordination separate Moses from the Israelite people, albeit in different ways. The divine election in the priestly literature accentuates the separation of Moses from the Israelites to a priestly office that is sacerdotal in nature, in which Moses functions as an ambassador of God who mediates holiness through rituals. The people's selection of Moses in Deuteronomy arises from the holiness of the whole people of God, who hear the voice of God, see the charismatic gifts in Moses, and elect him to a functional ordination of service as the one who will teach the divine word to them. Thus, the prophetic ordination of Moses emphasizes more the process of his position, while the priestly literature accentuates the rite of ordination as a choice of the deity. The Mosaic office requires the ordained to relate the two poles of prophet and priest in a creative tension. The tension suggests that an important feature of ministerial identity is not to determine *whether* ordination is sacerdotal or functional, but *when* the power of holiness is best accessed through sacramental rituals or through the charismatic teaching of the divine word at different occasions in ministry.

The Mosaic Office and the Ecumenical Mandate

The Faith and Order Paper on Baptism, Eucharist, and Ministry presents an ecumenical mandate for the mutual recognition of ordained ministry throughout the various forms of Christian tradition. The report concludes that ordained ministry is "constitutive for the life and witness of the Church" and that the theological understanding of ordination is crucial for vocational identity and for any progress toward the mutual recognition of the ordained in ecumenical dialogue. As a result, the report urges all churches to "examine the forms of ordained ministry and the degree to which [they] are faithful to its original intentions." "Churches," the report concludes, "must be prepared to renew their understanding and their practice of ordained ministry as they enter into ecumenical dialogue."[20] The methodology of canonical criticism provides a hermeneutical approach for interpreting the Mosaic office, which satisfies the ecumenical mandate of the World Council of Churches, since it assumes the mutual influence of denominations and communities of faith upon one another in fashioning a broad theology of ordination within Christian tradition.

A Canonical Interpretation of Holiness and Ordination

We have seen that there is an abundant quality to holiness in biblical literature. The result is that descriptions of the relationship between the sacred and the profane and the nature of ordination exceed the limits of any one theory. Biblical authors sought to capture the plentiful nature of the sacred by describing two theories of holiness, as a dynamic power and as a ritual resource, which give rise to the distinct forms of prophetic and priestly ordination within the Mosaic office. The ordination to the word and sacrament in Christian tradition continues the tradition of the biblical authors, since the categories of ordination also arise from the dual character of holiness. We have also seen that the two characteristics of holiness and the two forms of ordination cannot be harmonized with each other but must, instead, be held in tension.

The challenge for a biblical theology of ordination is to maintain the expansive quality of holiness by affirming both the prophetic and the priestly aspects of the Mosaic office. The tendency in the history of the church has been to emphasize one aspect of ordination over the other in the formation of distinct denominations and thus to weaken the power of holiness in the profession of ordination and in the life of the people of God. Canonical criticism provides a way to move toward embracing both the prophetic and priestly dimensions of ordination, without harmonizing the two offices and thus restricting the distinctive power of holiness as both a dynamic power and a ritual resource. Our review of canonical criticism will be separated into two parts. A summary of the social and theological challenges of the modern and postmodern eras of biblical interpretation will lay the groundwork for exploring the goals of a canonical interpretation of ordination within the Mosaic office.

THE SOCIAL AND THEOLOGICAL BACKGROUND FOR THE RISE OF CANONICAL CRITICISM. The modern and postmodern study of biblical literature confronts us with two fundamental challenges in fashioning a biblical theology of ordination for all people, in all places, and at all times. The two related problems are the lack of theological unity to biblical literature and the diverse communities of faith that read and hear scripture differently in light of their unique social and religious experiences.

The rise of historical criticism in the modern period uncovered the multiple, historically conditioned, and conflicting voices within the Bible. We have noted this in passing in our study of the Mosaic office. The prophetic and priestly idealizations of Moses were composed by different authors, who presented distinct theologies of God, worship, and ordination. The prophetic and priestly traditions represented by these authors likely competed with each other for authority in the developing history of ancient Israel. A primary focus of interpretation in the modern era has been to separate the distinct voices in order to recover the competing traditions in the history of ancient Israel. The fragmentation of scripture into multiple authors and competing traditions presents a direct challenge to the belief that scripture contains one authoritative word of God with regard to ordination.

The hermeneutical problem for fashioning a biblical theology of ordination throughout the modern period has been to reconcile the multiple voices of scripture into a single divine truth. Is there a center to canon with regard to the teaching on ordination? If there is not a theological center, should the interpreter pick one biblical voice over others, and thus create a canon within the canon, emphasizing either the prophetic or the priestly office of ordination over the other? The lingering problem with this solution is that the very authority of canon is lost if the interpreter can pick and choose favorite texts while ignoring others. The modern period of biblical interpretation has accentuated the pluralism within scripture and thus pressed the question of how interpreters are able to hear the voice of the same God through the historically dissimilar traditions of the prophetic and priestly accounts of the Mosaic office.

The postmodern period of interpretation has intensified the problem of an authoritative canon by introducing the formative role of experience in the appropriation of scripture as the word of God. The modern period confronted the interpreter with the multiple voices within the canon, which could not be harmonized into a single truth. Yet, in the modern period, interpreters held to the ideal that multiple readers of the same text could arrive at a similar interpretation through agreed-upon methodologies. Interpreters in the postmodern period have removed even this limited view of hermeneutical unity by stressing the formative role of experience in interpretation, which prompts distinct communities to read the same text in different ways. In the postmodern period, factors such as social location have fragmented interpretation even further. A Presbyterian will interpret the Mosaic office differently than a Lutheran, or Episcopalian, or Catholic. The postmodern period of biblical interpretation has accentuated the pluralism of the readers and hearers of scripture in addition to the multiple voices within canon. The formative role of experience in the interpretation of any text has intensified the problem of fashioning a comprehensive biblical theology of ordination, since the canon is no longer viewed as containing a single truth.

THE GOALS OF CANONICAL CRITICISM. Canonical criticism addresses the authority of scripture in a pluralistic world. Brevard S. Childs pro-

vided guidelines for the interpreter to reevaluate the nature of an authoritative canon, not as representing a single truth, but as providing the
boundaries of truth. James. A. Sanders explored the dynamic relationship
between a fixed canon and the ever-changing communities of faith,
which appropriate and adapt scripture through their unique experiences.
The dynamic character of canonical criticism provides a road map for
embracing both the prophetic and priestly dimensions of the Mosaic
office, while honoring the rich diversity of ordination in Christian
tradition.

Childs opened a new phase in the theological interpretation of
scripture by focusing on the genre of canon. He argued that the interweaving of the two aspects of the Mosaic office into a single story of
Moses indicates that the Torah is meant to represent a biblical theology of
controlled pluralism. The historical-critical period of interpretation
firmly established the theological pluralism represented by the authors of
Torah. The multiple voices in Torah provided the starting point for
Childs. His focus, however, was not on the distinct traditions, but on
their present relationship in the formation of a religiously authoritative
canon.[21] Thus, the Mosaic office is a chorus of voices and not a solo
performance; it provides the boundaries of possible interpretations of
ordination, rather than one truth.

Childs looked for literary features in the shape of canon, which
provide the reader with a road map of how to bring historically dissimilar
traditions into a holistic reading. Historical-critical interpretation of the
political setting of the authors aids in identifying the parts of the Mosaic
office, and it even safeguards against an artificial unity to the literature.
But the poetics of canon looks for the relationship of the distinctive
voices within the Mosaic office, in which historically dissimilar texts
qualify and complement each other to create a large literary corpus.[22]
Thus, an interpretation of the social and political backgrounds of
the distinct authors of the story of Moses does not adequately interpret
the Mosaic office in its present canonical shape. The interpreter of the
Mosaic office must also explore the literary features which combine the
prophetic and priestly portrayals of Moses into a single complex corpus.

Sanders's interpretation of canon branched out in a different direction to explore in more detail the function of canon within faith
communities. Thus, in contrast to Childs, who concentrated on the
unique literary features within canon, Sanders focused on the identities
of the communities of faith that embrace the canon through time in

different social contexts. Sanders wanted to know how a fixed, stable text, like a closed canon, was able to remain dynamic and adaptable through time. The adaptability of canon lies in its reuse by the ever-changing communities of faith, which seek identity and an ethical vision from its stories.[23]

When the Torah, with its portrayal of the Mosaic office, is embraced as the authoritative word of God, a community of faith cannot help but adapt the message to its particular social setting and life experience. In the process, the Torah becomes a "book of life."[24] The portrayal of ordination in the Mosaic office remains constant in Torah, but it takes on the color and the hues of the community that has chosen to remember the Torah and to live by the theology of ordination in the Mosaic office. Thus, the one story of the Mosaic office will be adapted in different ways by Catholic, Methodist, or Baptist communities of faith as they fashion a biblical theology of ordination within the context of their distinctive traditions. The formative role of experience in the interpretation of the Mosaic office results in a broad pluralism in the understanding of ordination within distinct faith communities. The pluralism is inevitable, even though different faith communities read the same text, because the priestly and the prophetic aspects of the Mosaic office are made to conform to different traditions of faith.

Two important qualities characterize any faith community that lives by canon and embraces the authoritative portrayal of Moses. The first is that both the prophetic and the priestly aspects of the Mosaic office must be related in some fashion within a theology of word and sacrament. The second is social harmony and peace—qualities that Sanders describes as the quest to "monotheize."[25] Social harmony and peace arise from the recognition that the multiple relationships between the prophetic and priestly aspects of the Mosaic office will always exceed any one inter-pretation by a particular community of faith, which therefore requires an ecumenical perspective with regard to a biblical theology of ordination. The result is that no Christian faith community or denomination will hold the monopoly on the exact relationship of the prophetic and priestly aspects of ordination to the Mosaic office.

Canonical criticism allows for a biblical theology of ordination in a pluralistic world. It frees the interpreter from searching for a single unifying message either in the canon or in Christian tradition, because it rejects the notion of a single meaning to scripture. A canonical inter-pretation recognizes the prophetic and priestly aspects of the Mosaic office, but does not interpret them as being in conflict with each other nor as having only one characteristic relationship. Rather, the two aspects define the boundaries of ordination and the parameters of a multitude of relationships. The power of ordination is unleashed in its fullest potential when the poles of the prophetic and the priestly ordinations are understood to yield a variety of different relationships in the one Mosaic office. In this way, a canonical interpretation of the Mosaic office maintains the expansive quality of holiness by affirming both the prophetic and the priestly aspects of the Mosaic office, without harmonizing the two forms of ministry or predetermining their exact relationship.

The challenge of a canonical interpretation of the Mosaic office for distinct Christian traditions is to embrace the full range of holiness that is available through ordination, even though the community of faith may favor one aspect of the Mosaic office over another. Denominations that favor the charismatic power of holiness in the ordination to the divine word will be challenged to recognize the ritual power of holiness in the priestly office, while the more priestly-oriented traditions of ordination will need to explore the charismatic resource of holiness. In this way, canonical criticism is able to provide a way forward, embracing both the prophetic and priestly dimensions of ordination without harmonizing the two offices and thus without restricting the distinctive power of holiness as a dynamic power and as a ritual resource. In place of a forced and artificial unity or the fragmentation of holiness, canonical criticism advocates a range of authoritative interpretations of ordination, which are able to support a broad diversity of Christian traditions.

The Mutual Recognition of the Ordained in Ecumenical Dialogue

The canonical interpretation of the Mosaic office provides a framework for achieving mutual understanding of ordination in ecumenical dialogue, which is called for in *The Faith and Order Paper on Baptism, Eucharist, and Ministry*. At the core of the Mosaic office is the recognition that ordination includes both prophetic and priestly aspects, which can neither be harmonized nor separated from each other. The dynamic and essential relationship between the prophetic and the priestly aspects of the Mosaic office provides the springboard for a broad ecumenical biblical theology of ordination, which also allows for the distinctive forms of ordination in Christian tradition. The key for an ecumenical interpretation is to reject the temptation to pick the prophetic or the priestly aspect of the Mosaic office over the other and instead to ground an interpretation of ordination in a relational view of the power of holiness as both a dynamic force and a ritual resource.

Bernard Loomer defines relational power as "the ability both to produce and to undergo an effect." It is to be contrasted to a unilateral view of power, which Loomer defines as "the ability to produce intended or desired effects on the other."[26] An interpretation of ordination which picks either the prophetic or the priestly dimension of the Mosaic office at the exclusion of the other would represent a unilateral interpretation of holiness. A unilateral interpretation of ordination could be prophetic or priestly, functional or sacramental, but not both. Such an interpretation of ordination embraces only one dimension of holiness at the exclusion of the other, and it is often accompanied by a defense of the superiority of its reading over all others. One social implication of the unilateral interpretation of ordination is the fragmentation of Christian tradition into distinct communities of faith representing only partial reflections of holiness either as a dynamic force or as a ritual resource. The unilateral interpretation of ordination represents a weakened form of holiness, regardless of how intensively any particular community of faith adheres to it, since it inevitably restricts the full power of holiness. The result is a fragmentary form of pluralism, which lacks dynamic ecumenical relationships.

The Mosaic office advocates a relational view of the power of holiness in the interpretation of ordination. A relational interpretation of the Mosaic office does not deny the preference of the prophetic or priestly dimensions of ordination by different communities of faith. In fact, a preference for one aspect of the Mosaic office is necessary for a relational interpretation of ordination to acquire strength. The difference between a unilateral and a relational interpretation of the Mosaic office is that the goal of interpretation is not to defend one aspect of ordination over another, but to fashion a relationship between the prophetic and the priestly roles of ordination, which can only be accomplished through ecumenical dialogue coupled with a mutual understanding of ordination. In this way, distinctive communities of faith seek to appropriate the full range of holiness through ecumenical dialogue, even though they may prefer one form of holiness and ordination over the other. A strong interpretation of ordination would be measured by the degree to which any particular denomination is able to incorporate the aspect of the

Mosaic office which they instinctively reject. A relational interpretation of ordination acquires strength within a pluralistic context through the active engagement of differing interpretations in ecumenical dialogue. Such an understanding and approach to ordination realizes that the expansive power of holiness exceeds the limits of any particular community.

The Mosaic Office and the Ordination to a Particular Denomination

The interpretation of the Mosaic office provides a framework for a theological understanding of ordination to word and sacrament. It does not provide a specific theology of ordination for any particular Christian community or denomination. We have seen in our study of the offices in the New Testament that Christian theologies of ordination took shape more in the period of church history than in the period of the emerging church as it is represented in the New Testament. The theological reflection on ordination has continued to develop in a dynamic way throughout the history of the church and into the present time. For this reason, all theologies of ordination must be fashioned in light of the official statements of particular denominations. But, as noted by Stephen V. Sprinkle, denominational statements on ordination often ground their theology of ordination in scripture.[27]

The purpose of this study of the prophetic and priestly aspects of the Mosaic office has been to provide a helpful template for evaluating the interpretation of ordination within any specific Christian tradition. The comparison of the statements on ordination in any denomination with the broad outline of ordination that is developed in the Mosaic office is meant to aid candidates for ordained ministry to word and sacrament, who are examining "the forms of ordained ministry and the degree to which the churches are faithful to its original intentions."[28]

RESOURCES FOR FURTHER STUDY

Campbell, D. M. *Yoke of Obedience: The Meaning of Ordination in Methodism.* Nashville, Tenn.: Abingdon, 1988.

Childs, B. S. *Introduction to the Old Testament as Scripture.* Philadelphia: Fortress, 1979.

———. *Biblical Theology of the Old and New Testaments*. Philadelphia: Fortress, 1993.

Gregory, L., and K. R. Armstrong. *Resurrecting Excellence: Shaping Faithful Christian Ministry*. Grand Rapids, Mich.: Eerdmans, 2006.

John Paul II. *Gift and Mystery: On the Fiftieth Anniversary of My Priestly Ordination*. New York: Doubleday, 1999.

Lathrop, G. W. *The Pastor: A Spirituality*. Minneapolis, Minn.: Fortress, 2006.

Niebuhr, H. Richard. *The Purpose of the Church and Its Ministry*. New York: Harper and Row, 1956.

Nouwen, H. J. M. *In the Name of Jesus: Reflections on Christian Leadership*. New York: Crossroads, 1989.

Sanders, J. A. *Torah and Canon*. Philadelphia: Fortress, 1972.

———. *Canon as Paradigm: From Sacred Story to Sacred Text*. Philadelphia: Fortress, 1987.

Sprinkle, S. *Ordination: Celebrating the Gift of Ministry*. St. Louis, Mo.: Chalice, 2004.

Taylor, B. Brown. *Leaving Church: A Memoir of Faith*. San Francisco, Calif.: Harper, 2006.

"Vocation" (special issue). *Interpretation: A Journal of Bible and Theology* 59, no. 2 (April 2005).

Willimon, W. H. *Pastor: The Theology and Practice of Ordained Ministry*. Nashville, Tenn.: Abingdon, 2002.

Witham, L. *Who Shall Lead Them? The Future of Ministry in America*. New York: Oxford University Press, 2005.

Notes

CHAPTER I

1. F. A. M. Wiggermann, "Theologies, Priests, and Worship in Ancient Mesopotamia," in *Civilizations of the Ancient Near East*, vol. 3, ed. J. M. Sasson (New York: Scribner's, 1995), pp. 1857–70.

2. H. Te Velde, "Theology, Priests, and Worship in Ancient Egypt," in *Civilizations of the Ancient Near East*, vol. 3, ed. J. M. Sasson (New York: Scribner's, 1995), pp. 1731–49.

3. K. Van Der Toorn, "Theology, Priests, and Worship in Canaan and Ancient Israel," in *Civilizations of the Ancient Near East*, vol. 3, ed. J. M. Sasson (New York: Scribner's, 1995), pp. 2043–58.

4. L. A. Witham, *Who Shall Lead Them? The Future of Ministry in America* (New York: Oxford University Press, 2005), p. 1.

5. H. J. M. Nouwen, *In the Name of Jesus: Reflections on Christian Leadership* (New York: Crossroads, 1989), pp. 65–66.

6. *The Faith and Order Paper on Baptism, Eucharist, and Ministry* (Geneva: World Council of Churches, 1982), p. 32 (hereafter *BEM*).

7. *BEM*, p. 32.

8. S. V. Sprinkle, *Ordination: Celebrating the Gift of Ministry* (St. Louis, Mo.: Chalice, 2004).

9. Sprinkle, *Ordination*, p. 43.

10. M. Eliade, *The Sacred and the Profane: The Nature of Religion* (New York: Harcourt, 1957).

11. R. Otto, *The Idea of the Holy: An Inquiry into the Non-Rational Factor in the Idea of the Divine and Its Relation to the Rational*, 2nd ed., trans. J. W. Harvey (Oxford: Oxford University Press, 1917).

12. J. Milgrom, *Leviticus 1–16: A New Translation with Introduction and Commentary* (Anchor Bible 3A; Garden City, N.Y.: Doubleday, 1991); Mil-

grom, *Leviticus 17–22: A New Translation with Introduction and Commentary* (Anchor Bible 3A; Garden City, N.Y.: Doubleday, 2000); and Milgrom, *Leviticus 23–27: A New Translation with Introduction and Commentary* (Anchor Bible 3B; Garden City, N.Y.: Doubleday, 2001).

13. For summaries of the history of the composition of the Pentateuch, see J. J. Collins, *Introduction to the Hebrew Bible* (Minneapolis, Minn.: Fortress, 2004); J. Blenkinsopp, *The Pentateuch: An Introduction to the First Five Books of the Bible* (Garden City, N.Y.: Doubleday, 1992); A. F. Campbell and M. A. O'Brien, *Sources of the Pentateuch: Texts, Introductions, and Annotations* (Minneapolis, Minn.: Fortress, 1993); M. Noth, *A History of Pentateuchal Traditions*, trans. B. W. Anderson (Englewood Cliffs, N.J.: Prentice-Hall, 1971); and J. Wellhausen, *Prolegomena to the History of Ancient Israel*, trans. A. Menzies and J. S. Black (1883; Reprint, New York: Meridian, 1957).

14. For a similar interpretation of Moses, which focuses more on his office and the personification of authority, see D. Allison, *The New Moses: A Matthean Typology* (Minneapolis, Minn.: Fortress, 1993). For an interpretation of the character of Moses as opposed to a study of authoritative office, see J. Lierman, *The New Testament Moses: Christian Perceptions of Moses and Israel in the Setting of Jewish Religion* (Tuebingen: Mohr Siebeck, 2004).

15. See, for example, Lierman (*The New Testament Moses*, pp. 79–174), who also identifies images of Moses as king and as lawgiver in the composition of the New Testament.

16. B. S. Childs, *The Book of Exodus: A Critical, Theological Commentary* (Old Testament Library; Philadelphia: Westminster, 1974); Childs, *Introduction to the Old Testament as Scripture* (Philadelphia: Fortress, 1979); Childs, *Old Testament Theology in a Canonical Context* (Minneapolis, Minn.: Fortress, 1985); Childs, *Biblical Theology of the Old and New Testaments* (Philadelphia: Fortress, 1993); J. A. Sanders, *Torah and Canon* (Philadelphia: Fortress, 1972); and Sanders, *Canon as Paradigm: From Sacred Story to Sacred Text* (Philadelphia: Fortress, 1987).

17. Childs, *Old Testament Theology in a Canonical Context*, p. 6.

18. Sanders, *Canon as Paradigm*, pp. 65–66.

19. My study of the portrayal of Moses is also confined to the Hebrew Bible. The result is that the rich literary portrayal of Moses in the late second temple period will not be a focus of study here, even though these portrayals certainly influenced the composition of the New Testament literature. See, for example, Allison, *The New Moses*; Lierman, *The New Testament Moses*; and J. Gager, *Moses in Greco-Roman Paganism* (Atlanta, Ga.: Scholars, 1972).

20. G. T. Sheppard, "Canonization: Hearing the Voice of the Same God through Historically Dissimilar Traditions," *Interpretation* 36 (1982): 21–33.

21. Childs, *Introduction to the Old Testament as Scripture*, p. 83.

22. Sanders, *Canon as Paradigm*, pp. 65–66.

CHAPTER 2

1. Milgrom, *Leviticus 17–22*, p. 1712.

2. D. P. Wright, "Holiness," In *The Anchor Bible Dictionary*, vol. 3; ed. D. N. Freedman (New York: Doubleday, 1992), pp. 237–49. For additional reflection on holiness, see John G. Gammie, *Holiness in Israel* (Overtures to Biblical Theology; Minneapolis, Minn.: Augsburg Fortress, 1989); and Stephen C. Barton (ed.), *Holiness Past and Present* (London: Clark, 2003).

3. See Milgrom, *Leviticus 1–16*, pp. 42–61, 616.

4. Eliade, *The Sacred and the Profane*, p. 14.

5. See Milgrom, *Leviticus 1–16*, pp. 718–36, 1000–1009.

6. Milgrom, *Leviticus 1–16*, p. 616.

7. G. E. Mendenhall, *The Tenth Generation: The Origins of the Biblical Tradition* (Baltimore, Md.: Johns Hopkins University Press, 1973), pp. 32–66.

8. Otto, *The Idea of the Holy*, pp. 5–30. Otto concludes that holiness as the numinous is pre-moral.

9. For discussion on the fear of the holy (or numinous), see Otto, *The Idea of the Holy*, pp. 25–30.

10. R. E. Clements, *God and Temple* (Philadelphia: Fortress, 1965), p. 2.

11. There remains a tension surrounding the relationship of holiness and sanctuaries in the Bible. The biblical writers take care to underscore that holiness cannot be imprisoned in a sanctuary. The confinement of holiness to the temple is a lie according to the prophet Jeremiah. The fall of the Jerusalem temple was a painful lesson to the prophet Ezekiel that the glory of Yahweh was free to leave the temple. The priestly author of the Pentateuch agrees, noting that the glory of Yahweh is able to leave the Tabernacle in order to lead the people in their wilderness pilgrimage. And the New Testament writers emphasize that the Holy Spirit blows freely in the world.

12. A. van Gennep, *The Rites of Passage*, trans. M. B. Vizedon and G. L. Caffee (1908; Chicago: University of Chicago Press, 1960).

13. Van Gennep (*The Rites of Passage*, p. 21) describes the three phases of the rite of passage as (1) preliminal, the separation from a previous world; (2) liminal, the rites executed during the transitional state; and (3) postliminal, ceremonies of incorporation into the new world.

14. V. Turner, *The Ritual Process: Structure and Anti-Structure* (New York: Aldine de Gruyter, 1969), pp. 94–96.

15. V. Turner and E. Turner, *Image and Pilgrimage in Christian Culture: Anthropological Perspectives* (New York: Columbia University Press, 1978), p. 249.

16. Otto, *The Idea of the Holy*, pp. 5–6.

17. Otto, *The Idea of the Holy*, pp. 25–30, 61.

18. Otto, *The Idea of the Holy*, pp. 60–61.

19. Otto, *The Idea of the Holy*, p. 8.

20. Otto, *The Idea of the Holy*, p. 75.

21. M. Weber, *Theory of Social and Economic Organization*, trans. A. M. Henderson and T. Parsons (New York: Oxford University Press, 1947), p. 358; Weber, *On Charisma and Institution Building*, ed. S. N. Eisenstadt (Chicago: University of Chicago Press, 1968); Weber, *Ancient Judaism*, trans. H. H. Gerth and D. Matindale (New York: Free Press, 1952), pp. 11–23; Weber, "The Prophet," in *Prophecy in Israel: Search for an Identity*, ed. D. L. Petersen (Philadelphia: Fortress, 1987), pp. 99–111.

22. Milgrom, *Leviticus 17–22*, p. 1606.

23. Milgrom, *Leviticus 1–16*, pp. 42–47; Milgrom, *Leviticus 17–22*, p. 1398; and Milgrom, "The Changing Concept of Holiness in the Pentateuchal Codes with Emphasis on Leviticus 19," in *Reading Leviticus: A Conversation with Mary Douglas*, ed. John F. A. Sawyer (Journal for the Study of the Old Testament Supplement Series 227; Sheffield, England: Sheffield Academic, 1996), pp. 65–75.

24. Milgrom, *Leviticus 1–16*, p. 569.

25. Milgrom, *Leviticus 1–16*, pp. 616–17, 732–73, 977; and Milgrom, "The Changing Concept of Holiness," pp. 65–66.

26. Milgrom, *Leviticus 1–16*, pp. 730–31; Milgrom, *Leviticus 17–22*, p. 1398; Milgrom, "The Changing Concept of Holiness," pp. 65–67.

27. Milgrom, *Leviticus 1–16*, pp. 718–36.

28. Milgrom, "The Changing Concept of Holiness," p. 66.

29. Milgrom, *Leviticus 1–16*, p. 53.

30. Milgrom, *Leviticus 1–16*, p. 524.

31. Milgrom, *Leviticus 1–16*, p. 498; *Babylonian Talmud, Zevahim*, 17b.

CHAPTER 3

1. S. Terrien, *The Elusive Presence: Toward a New Biblical Theology* (New York: Harper and Row, 1978), p. 70.

2. S. Dean McBride, "Transcendent Authority: The Role of Moses in Old Testament Traditions," *Interpretation* 44 (1990): 229–39.

3. Childs, *Exodus*, pp. 260, 324, 351–60.

4. Childs, *Exodus*, p. 501

5. Childs, *Exodus*, p. 368.

6. See n. 13, chapter 2.

7. Herodotus, *Histories* 1.107–30.

8. James B. Pritchard, *Ancient Near Eastern Texts Relating to the Old Testament* (2nd ed.; Princeton: Princeton University Press, 1969), p. 119.

9. B. Lewis, *The Sargon Legend* (American Schools of Oriental Research Dissertation Series 4; Cambridge: American Schools of Oriental Research, 1980), p. 249.

10. Childs, *Exodus*, p. 9.

11. W. Propp, *Exodus 1–18* (Anchor Bible 2A; Garden City, N.Y.: Doubleday, 1999), p. 158.

12. Turner, *The Ritual Process*, pp. 94–96.

13. T. B. Dozeman, "Creation and Environment in the Character Development of Moses," in *Character Ethics and the Old Testament: Moral Dimensions of Scripture*, ed. M. Daniel, R. Carroll, and J. E. Lapsley (Louisville, Ky.: Westminster/John Knox, 2007), pp. 27–36.

14. T. B. Dozeman, "Masking Moses and Mosaic Authority in Torah," *Journal of Biblical Literature* 119 (2000): 21–45.

15. M. Aberbach and L. Smolar, "Aaron, Jeroboam, and the Golden Calves," *Journal of Biblical Literature* 86 (1967): 129–40.

16. *Mishnah Avot* 5:18. See also 2 Pt 2:15.

17. Otto, *The Idea of the Holy*, pp. 60–61.

18. Eliade, *The Sacred and the Profane*, p. 14.

19. N. Habel, "The Form and Significance of the Call Narratives," *Zeitschrift für die Alttestamentliche Wissenschaft* 77 (1965): 297–323.

20. E. Auerbach, *Mimesis: The Representation of Reality in Western Literature*, trans. W. R. Trask (Princeton, N.J.: Princeton University Press, 1968), pp. 3–23.

21. Milgrom, *Leviticus 17–22*, p. 1606.

22. W. Zimmerli, "I Am Yahweh," in *I Am Yahweh*, trans. D. W. Stott (Atlanta, Ga.: John Knox, 1982), pp. 1–28.

23. N. Sarna, *Exodus: The JPS Torah Commentary* (Philadelphia: Jewish Publication Society, 1991), p. 31.

CHAPTER 4

1. D. Olson, *Deuteronomy and the Death of Moses: A Theological Reading* (Overtures to Biblical Theology; Minneapolis, Minn.: Fortress, 1994), describes the book of Deuteronomy as the last will and testament of Moses from his final day of life on earth.

2. Otto, *The Idea of the Holy*, p. 168.

3. Otto, *The Idea of the Holy*, p. 83.

4. Otto, *The Idea of the Holy*, pp. 82–83; p. 87.

5. Otto, *The Idea of the Holy*, pp. 177–78.

6. Otto, *The Idea of the Holy*, p. 171.

CHAPTER 5

1. B. A. Levine, *The JPS Torah Commentary: Leviticus: The Traditional Hebrew Text with the New JPS Translation* (Philadelphia: Jewish Publication Society, 1989), p. 216.

2. R. B. Y. Scott, "A Kingdom of Priests (Exodus XIX 6)," *Oudtestamentische Studien* 8 (1950): 213–19; W. L. Moran, "A Kingdom of Priests," in *The Bible in Current Catholic Thought*, ed. J. L. McKenzie (New York: Herder and Herder, 1962), pp. 7–20; and Childs, *The Book of Exodus*, p. 367.

3. P. P. Jensen, *Graded Holiness: A Key to the Priestly Conception of the World* (Sheffield, England: Sheffield Academic, 1992).

4. J. Marcus, *Mark 1–8* (Anchor Bible 27A; Garden City, N.Y.: Doubleday, 2000).

CHAPTER 6

1. A. Stewart-Sykes, *On the Apostolic Tradition: Hippolytus* (Crestwood, N.Y.: St. Vladimir's Seminary Press, 2002).

2. *BEM*, p. 24.

CHAPTER 7

1. Eliade, *The Sacred and the Profane*, p. 14.

2. Otto, *The Idea of the Holy*, pp. 5–30.

3. Milgrom, *Leviticus 1–16*, pp. 42–47, 569.

4. See D. M. Campbell, *Who Will Go for Us? An Invitation to Ordained Ministry* (Nashville, Tenn.: Abingdon, 1994), pp. 86–89.

5. Van Gennep, *The Rites of Passage*, p. 21.

6. Campbell, *Who Will Go for Us?* p. 89.

7. Otto, *The Idea of the Holy*, pp. 5–6, 25–30. See chapter 2 for further discussion.

8. Weber, *On Charisma and Institution Building*.

9. Milgrom, *Leviticus 1–16*, pp. 718–36. See chapter 2 for further discussion.

10. *BEM*, pp. 20–27.

11. Sprinkle, *Ordination*, p. 13.

12. H. Richard Niebuhr, *The Purpose of the Church and Its Ministry* (New York: Harper and Row, 1956), p. 64.

13. W. H. Willimon, *Pastor: The Theology and Practice of Ordained Ministry* (Nashville, Tenn.: Abingdon, 2002), p. 40.

14. *BEM*, p. 22.

15. *BEM*, pp. 21–22.

16. See, for example, *The Christian as Minister: An Exploration into the Meaning of God's Call* (Nashville, Tenn.: General Board of Higher Education and Ministry, United Methodist Church, 2006), pp. 15–19.

17. Nouwen, *In the Name of Jesus*, pp. 65–66.

18. Sprinkle, *Ordination*, pp. 17–61.

19. Sprinkle, *Ordination*, p. 15. Sprinkle offers the analogy of different tunings of a stringed instrument to achieve different harmonies.

20. *BEM*, p. 32.

21. Childs, *Introduction to the Old Testament as Scripture*, p. 82.

22. Childs, *Introduction to the Old Testament as Scripture*, pp. 71–87.

23. Sanders, *Canon as Paradigm*, pp. 65–66.

24. Sanders, *Canon as Paradigm*, pp. 5–6.

25. Sanders, *Canon as Paradigm*, p. xii.

26. Bernard Loomer, "Two Kinds of Power," *Criterion* 15 (1976): 11–29, esp. 14, 20.

27. Sprinkle, *Ordination*, p. 43.

28. *BEM*, p. 32.

Scripture Index

Author Index

Subject Index